little
LONE STAR
quilts

- Sew Perfect Points Every Time

- Exciting New Paper-Piecing Technique

- 7 Projects

LORRAINE OLSEN

C&T PUBLISHING

Text copyright © 2009 by Lorraine Olsen

Artwork copyright © 2009 by C&T Publishing, Inc.

Publisher: Amy Marson

Creative Director: Gailen Runge

Editors: Sasha Nelson and Kesel Wilson

Technical Editors: Carolyn Aune and Ann Haley

Copyeditor/Proofreader: Wordfirm Inc.

Cover/Book Designer: Kristen Yenche

Page Layout Artist: Happenstance Type-O-Rama

Production Coordinator: Zinnia Heinzmann

Illustrator: Tim Manibusan

Photography by Christina Carty-Francis and Diane Pedersen of C&T Publishing, Inc., unless otherwise noted.

Published by C&T Publishing, Inc., P.O. Box 1456, Lafayette, CA 94549

Library of Congress Cataloging-in-Publication Data

Olsen, Lorraine

Little lone star quilts : sew perfect points every time : exciting new paper-piecing technique, 7 projects / Lorraine Olsen.

p. cm.

Summary: "Revolutionary sew-and-fold paper piecing quilting method for creating miniature stars. Fast and timesaving technique means no need to measure or cut precisely. 7 projects, step-by-step instructions, and helpful troubleshooting chapter included"--Provided by publisher.

ISBN 978-1-57120-606-0 (paper trade : alk. paper)

1. Patchwork--Patterns. 2. Quilting--Patterns. 3. Star quilts. 4. Stars in art. I. Title.

TT835.O397 2009

746.46'041--dc22   2008050946

Printed in China

10 9 8 7 6 5 4 3 2 1

Acknowledgments

For the master craftswomen in my life, Yvonne, Bea, and Drucille, who taught me, inspired me, and allowed me the freedom to be creative.

Thanks to Julie, Patti, Demetria, Jane, Brandi, Leesa, Kristin, Laronda, Tracy, Missy, Cecile, Dianne, Sophia, Bob, and Emily for their generous help with supplies. Thanks to Yvonne for doing everything and more than I asked; to Debbie, Vickie, and Ann for their help, support, and enthusiasm; to Marilynn and Karen. Thanks to Sasha for her patience with this first-time author. Thanks to all the people at C&T, especially Kesel, Carolyn, Ann, Kristen, Zinnia, Tim, Gailen, and Amy. Thanks to Cullam and Roland for special editing help; to Christian, Brett, Janel, and Reed for computer help. Thanks to my family for all your patience, encouragement, and support.

contents

introduction

I love making miniatures; they are so cute. I still get a thrill when I open the last seam and see all the tiny points match up. I enjoy the challenge of figuring out how to make little quilts from classic patterns. It was a scrappy, antique, lone star quilt that first inspired me to create the paper fold-and-sew technique described in this book. The maker of this old quilt used a variety of fabrics to create an irregular, scrappy design instead of the more familiar pattern of concentric rings. Making the lone star pattern scrappy and small appealed to me.

I designed a lone star pattern with enough versatility to create many designs. The paper fold-and-sew technique starts with paper-pieced rows. The folded paper then perfectly matches the rows together. When each fabric piece is added individually, many designs in the pieced star points are possible. The design choices range from the traditional lone star pattern of concentric rings to a charm quilt with every diamond in the star a different fabric.

The instructions in this book offer basics for beginners and challenges for more experienced quilters. Those quilters who have never tried a miniature quilt will be surprised at how easy it is to create a mini masterpiece using the paper fold-and-sew technique. Miniature quilt artists will enjoy the ease of perfectly matched diamonds and the versatility of creating many designs in their lone star quilts.

The little stars with 1″ patches are great for learning my technique. The true miniature lone stars have diamond patches only ½″ in size and offer more of a challenge. Two larger star blocks are fun to try for those who just don't want to try a miniature quilt. Mix and match the five different borders with the star patterns in this book, or use the borders in other projects. Look for other creative ways to use the little stars, including in full-sized quilts, pillows, wallhangings, and bags.

Scrap quilts are a great way to show off a fabric collection. The energy, movement, and variety in a scrap quilt make it new and interesting with every viewing. A scrap quilt is unique to the maker, reflects favorite colors and fabrics, and is a history of past projects. Be creative with fabric, color, and design when making an original scrappy lone star quilt.

—Lorraine Olsen

tools and supplies

You will find most of the tools and supplies needed for making lone star blocks in a typical sewing room. Investing in a few additional supplies will ensure successful little quilts.

Basic Tools

Set up a workspace with a sewing machine, rotary cutting mat, and rulers. An open-toe presser foot on the sewing machine will allow for a better view of the sewing line when paper piecing. Some quilters like to use small tools to trim the seams when paper piecing; small rotary cutters and mats are not necessary for the projects in this book. Larger rulers provide a better grip, and the 45mm rotary cutter slices through the paper and fabric with ease. The ruler should have a clearly marked ¼″ line to accurately trim the completed star points and for squaring up the finished star blocks. Some projects require a ruler with a clearly marked 45° line.

Invest in a quality pair of small, sharp scissors. The small size makes them ideal for trimming seams and for trimming the completed rows. Large dressmaker shears are not accurate enough.

Use a fine-point mechanical pencil or a fine-line water erasable marker for marking the ¼″ seam lines on the background fabric. A narrow line is important for accurate piecing. A pair of tweezers is useful for removing the paper. Use a wooden iron or craft stick to fold the patterns and for finger pressing while paper piecing the rows. A small, sharp seam ripper is necessary for removing tiny stitches when correcting mistakes.

Other Important Tools

Binding Clips
Binding or hem clips are found in stores with the sewing notions and quilting supplies. Other stores sell the same product as hair clips. Binding clips are the ideal tool for holding paper-pieced star points together while stitching. They keep the pieces flat and do not distort the star points as pins do. Five or six binding clips are enough to complete the projects in this book.

Sewing Machine Needles
Small stars using ½″ or ¾″ diamond patches require a size 9 sewing machine needle. A size 10 or 11 needle is OK for stars using 1″ or 1¾″ diamond patches. A normal size 14 needle will destroy the fine pattern lines and will not be accurate enough to sew in the middle of the very fine lines on the pattern.

 tip Remember to change machine needles often. Sewing through paper will wear out a needle faster than sewing through fabric. If the needle is making a punching sound when stitching or the needle is pulling threads in the fabric, it is time for a needle change.

Thread
Fine, smooth 60-weight polyester thread is ideal for paper piecing these patterns because it is very fine and does not add bulk to the seam. It is also strong and does not stretch when removing the paper. This thread is available as bobbin thread at many quilt shops. Strong, smooth 50- or 60-weight cotton thread, found at quilt shops, is also satisfactory for paper piecing. Heavier-weight thread

will make the seam allowances bulky and the seam lines harder to match. You can stitch the larger stars with 1¾″ diamond patches with threads as heavy as 40- or 50-weight cotton.

Fabric Glue

Use a water-soluble fabric glue stick to attach fabric pieces to the paper patterns. The glue also holds down the fabric tails at the end of the rows. The glue stick package should say that the glue is easily removable with water.

 tip If the glue stick dries out, place it, with the cap off, in a zip-top bag along with a wet paper towel, and leave it for a day or two. The glue will become usable as it softens.

Pins

Use bridal or satin dressmaker pins with a fine shaft when joining the star points. Look for a shaft size of 0.5mm and a length over 1″. The fine points on these pins make a very small hole, and the long size makes the pins easy to remove. *Note: The photos in this book show larger size pins for better visibility only.*

Round-head quilting pins are not suitable for holding the star points together. The pin remains in the star points, perpendicular to the fabric, while you stitch the seam. The round head prevents the pieces from feeding flat into the sewing machine. Round-head or flat-head pins are suitable for other steps in the project.

Use size 9 machine needles, fine-weight thread such as Superior Bottom Line, dressmaker pins, fabric glue stick, binding clips, and small sharp scissors to complete projects successfully.

Paper

The paper used for making these projects should be sufficiently durable to withstand folding and sewing. It should also be lightweight enough to see the printed pattern easily from the back when the paper is held up to a window or bright light. There are both advantages and disadvantages to each different paper.

Computer Printer or Copy Paper

Computer printer paper or copy paper that is 20 lb. or lighter weight works well for the patterns in this book. It is inexpensive and widely available. It also creases easily and holds the fold well. The paper is durable if a seam needs to be picked out and resewn, and it tears away easily after the star block is completed. Computer paper is a good choice for a first project.

 tip Computer paper tears away more easily after it is immersed in water until completely damp and then left to dry. Test for bleeding of the ink on the fabric before getting the paper wet.

Computer printer or copy paper also has some disadvantages. The pattern may be hard to see from the back of the paper. Computer paper is bulky when joining the star points together, especially in the star center. Basting, as explained in Hand-Basting Method, page 23, will help with the bulky center. Computer paper may also allow the star points to slide around under the presser foot. Avoid this problem by basting the seams first or increasing the pressure on the presser foot.

Newsprint Paper

Newsprint paper, such as Carol Doak's Foundation Paper (available from C&T Publishing; see Resources, page 63), which is designed to work in a computer printer, is available at quilt shops and craft stores and is a good choice. Newsprint paper is flexible and easy to sew on. The star points do not slide around, and there is little bulk in the star center when using newsprint.

Newsprint paper does have some shortcomings when it is used for these patterns. The paper does not hold a crease as well as other papers. To avoid this problem, crease the folds very firmly with a wooden iron or a craft stick. Check to see that the crease has not shifted before stitching the fold seams. Newsprint paper tears easily when stitching is removed. Use less steam when pressing on newsprint to minimize crinkling the paper. Avoid newsprint paper for a first project or for the small stars with ½″ patches. It works well for the larger stars.

> Warning: Unlike computer paper, newsprint should not be immersed in water. This makes the paper harder to remove. First, tear away all the easy-to-remove paper. Then spray the paper that remains with a little water to release the glue. Let it dry before removing the remaining paper.

Vellum

Quilt shops and office supply stores carry vellum paper suitable for paper piecing. A good choice is Simple Foundations Translucent Vellum Paper (available from C&T Publishing; see Resources, page 63). Vellum is thin and easy to see through. It folds easily and holds a crease well. Vellum is very easy to remove after the star block is completed. When the star fabrics are dark, vellum is a good choice because the pattern is easily visible through the paper. Use acid-free vellum for any project where the paper will remain in the star. See the framed *Bride's Star*, page 45, for an example where acid-free vellum is the best choice.

Vellum has some qualities that make it difficult to use for the patterns in this book. Vellum is stiff and bulky in the star center when joining the star points together. Avoid this problem by basting the last two seams when sewing the star halves together, and sew from the inside corner to the star center. Vellum tears easily, so use a longer 1.5 stitch length when paper piecing. Use light steam and don't spray with water when pressing to avoid crinkling the paper.

Wash-Away Paper

Wash-away paper turns to a soft pulp that easily rinses away when it is wet. This paper, designed for computer printers, is available at quilt shops and fabric stores. Wash-away paper is transparent, so the pattern is easily visible from the back of the paper. It is thin and does not add bulk at the star center.

Because it is very difficult to pick out mistakes and correct them, wash-away paper is not a good choice for a first

project. Iron only very lightly on exposed wash-away paper, and do not use steam. The heat will scorch the paper and make it brittle. Finger press as much as possible, and iron the star points with the fabric side up. Remove as much paper as possible by gently tearing it away before immersing the star in water to remove the remaining paper.

From left to right: Newsprint paper, vellum, wash-away paper, and computer paper are all suitable for paper piecing the patterns in this book.

Copies and Ink

Computer printers, copiers, scanners, and commercial copy machines are all suitable for making multiple copies of the patterns required for each star. The quality of the ink and the precision of the copy can make a difference in the success of the completed project.

A computer inkjet or laser printer is a good choice for making copies. The lines print very thin and the copy is precise. Some commercial copy machines can distort the copy near the edge of the paper. When using any copying method, make sure the pattern is flat on the copier. Check the copy for distortion by comparing it with the original in the book, holding both up together to a bright light.

Ink and toner brands vary, and some may bleed when wet or steamed. Some may transfer to the fabric or to the iron when pressed. Be sure to test any printer ink or toner before using it with fabric. Print a test pattern, get the paper wet, and then press it with a hot iron. If the ink bleeds in this test, remove paper with printed lines before wetting your project, and do not use water or steam on the star points. If the ink or toner transfers or smudges when pressed, use a pressing cloth to protect the fabric and iron from the ink.

fabric

Choosing the right fabrics is important for a successful quilt. Fabric weight, print, color, and value all play a role in making a great star quilt. These projects are a good way to use small bits of fabric and show off a scrap collection. The quilts and blocks shown in this chapter will provide inspiration when you are making fabric choices.

Fabric Weight

Lightweight fabrics are essential for making these little stars. The pieces used to make little quilts are tiny, and the star patterns contain many seams. Batiks, muslin, and hand-dyed fabric are the perfect weight for the little star patterns. However, with any lightweight fabric, pay attention to fabric quality, and stay away from low-thread-count cottons, which will shred and unravel when stitched with a short stitch length.

Heavier-weight fabrics are not suitable. They will create bulky seams and make the intersections of the diamond patch seams difficult to match. Avoid fabrics that are too heavy to finger press easily.

 tip Pinch the fabric between your finger and fingernail. Fabric that does not crease easily is too heavy for these projects.

Fabric Print

The size, variety, and density of the print are important considerations when choosing fabric for quilts. Create visual interest by effectively combining a variety of print scales and print designs together in a project.

Print Scale

Print scale, or the size of the fabric print, is an important consideration. Use prints of different scales to make a quilt more interesting. Miniature stars require smaller prints for the motifs to show effectively in the tiny diamonds. Micro prints and textured fabrics are the right scale to act as small prints in miniature quilts. Use small- to medium-scale prints as the largest scale in miniature quilts.

Larger diamond patches in large 3-row star effectively show off collection of butterfly prints.

Save large-scale prints for the largest stars and for the backgrounds and borders of the small stars. The 1¾″ diamond patches in the large 3-row star are perfect for showing a collection of larger-scale prints.

Print Style

Block on left includes fabrics with different scales and styles together; block on right is made only of plaids.

Print styles include florals, checks, stripes, dots, geometrics, and novelty. Strive for interest by using a variety of styles in the same project. Try to include at least two different scales and at least three different styles.

Print Density

With this technique, it is difficult to fussy cut or place individual motifs to show in the diamond patches. For this reason, look for closely packed prints with very little open background. Otherwise, the little diamond patches could end up with all background and no print showing. Look for tightly packed prints in any scale. Even some large-scale prints with tightly packed motifs make interesting choices for small patches because it is difficult to predict what part of the print will fall within the diamond patch.

Fabrics with dense prints (top four) in any scale work well with these patterns. Avoid fabric with open backgrounds (bottom four).

 tip Make a viewing window by cutting the diamond patch shape into an index card. Pass the window over the fabric to check that the print design within the window looks interesting.

Fabric Color

There are many ways to choose the colors for a quilt. Every quilter has some favorites. Monochromatic quilts are those with only one color. Quilts with analogous color schemes use two or three colors that are closely related. Complementary colors are opposite each other on a color wheel. Develop confidence in trying other color schemes by using a color wheel or the *3-in-1 Color Tool* by Joen Wolfrom (available from C&T Publishing). Look for color inspiration in the world of nature, in advertising, and in fashion.

Different color combinations interpreted in lone star blocks: monochromatic (left), analogous (center), and complementary (right)

Using a pallet fabric is an easy way to choose quilt colors. The pallet fabric serves as a guide of colors that will harmonize well together. Choose the star colors from the colors in the fabric print, and use the pallet fabric as a background or border in the finished quilt.

Nursery print, used as background, serves as palette fabric for color choices of star points.

Fabric Value

Value is how light or dark a fabric *reads* when compared with the other fabrics in the quilt. A high contrast between the concentric rings creates a high-energy pulsing effect in the lone star design. A low contrast will create a calmer mood.

High contrast between concentric rings (left), and low contrast between concentric rings (right)

Value placement, rather than color, creates the design of concentric rings in *Rainy Day Star*, page 57, and the appearance of radiating points in *Charming Garden*.

In *Charming Garden*, dark floral prints on edges of star surround medium and light floral prints in star center.

To make an effective design using value, sort the fabrics into light, medium, and dark values. *Charming Garden* uses three values. Quilts like *Rainy Day Star* use five values: very light, light, medium, dark, and very dark. Use a design wall to sort the fabric pieces quickly without thinking too much.

 Make a design wall from a piece of foam core board covered with flannel or fleece. It is the perfect size for small quilts.

Sort in the evening or in poor light to help in ignoring the color. Take a photo to use as a record of the sorted piles for later reference.

Two 3-row star blocks made with five fabric values: lightest value in center and darkest value at tips. Neutrals used in left block are the same color, making it easier to sort for value. Disregard color when sorting fabrics for block at right.

 Check the sorted fabric with a digital or cell phone camera set to black and white. Pieces in the wrong pile will stand out quickly.

Using Scraps

It can be fun to use random scraps of any style, color, or value together in a lone star quilt like *Beggar's Star*, page 56. You can also sort and use fabric scraps in a more organized way, like in *Charming Garden*, which uses only floral prints sorted into three values.

Assorted '30s reproduction prints were used to make this quilt, but they are randomly placed with no attention to color or value.

Fabric scraps organized by color: prints with patriotic fabrics

Eighteenth-century reproduction prints

The stars in this book are all paper pieced, sometimes referred to as foundation pieced, and have backgrounds that are set in with Y seams. Those unfamiliar with these two procedures may wish to review a quilter's reference guide such as *All About Quilting from A to Z*, available from C&T Publishing, before beginning. The *North Star* quilt, page 34, is a good project on which to learn the paper fold-and-sew technique for those with little paper piecing experience. Quilters confident in their paper piecing skills can start with *Bea's Star*, page 42.

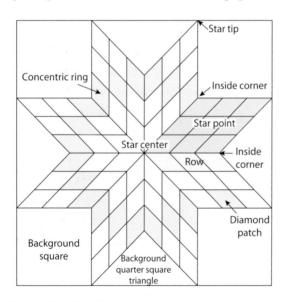

Parts of Lone Star block

The star patterns in this book simplify the complex lone star design, and the technique used avoids the careful measuring, precise cutting, and bias edges of other methods. However, the projects do require an attention to detail to complete the stars. Precisely follow the fold lines and the seam lines on the pattern to create perfectly matched points. *All solid lines on the patterns in this book are sewing lines. The fold lines are dashed.*

When making small and miniature quilts, it is easier to handle and correctly place *larger* pieces of fabric and then trim the fabric down. Oversized rectangles of fabric complete the diamond shapes. Oversized background fabrics allow extra for squaring up the completed block.

Unlike other paper-piecing patterns, the numbers on the pattern are *not* the order in which the pieces are added. The numbers represent the *color* of the fabric pieces. In this technique, arrows indicate the first patch to be pieced in each row and the order for piecing the remaining patches.

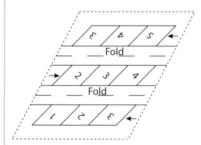

Pattern for a 3-row star

Each project has a layout and assembly diagram. The numbers printed on the paper patterns will make a design of concentric rings on the finished star. Use a copy of the layout diagram to work out the colors first with colored pencils before the sewing begins.

With the paper fold-and-sew technique, many design possibilities, other than concentric rings, are possible. Designs like the quilt *Charming Garden*, page 9, are easy to do. Work out any original design on the layout first. Use a pencil to mark on the patterns where each type of fabric will be sewn.

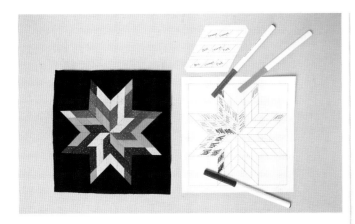
Work out layout first, and then transfer to paper pattern.

Preparing Patterns and Fabric

Before any sewing begins, make copies of the chosen pattern, fold the pattern copies, cut, and label the star fabrics.

Make Copies of Star Points Pattern

The patterns provided make a single star point. The lone star is an eight-pointed star, so eight copies of the pattern are required to make one star. To make the copies, use a copy machine or computer. See Tools and Supplies, page 4, for suggestions about paper and copying methods. *Do not trace the pattern.* It is not possible to trace the pattern with the accuracy required to make a successful star. Make a few extra copies in case of mistakes. Cut out the eight copies of the paper pattern on the cutting line with paper scissors. Do not worry about accuracy when cutting out the pattern.

Fold Copies of Star Points Pattern

Do not underestimate the importance of proper folding. Finishing with matching patches and points depends on accurate folding. The pattern lines are very thin, but it is important to fold on the very center of the fold line.

Hold the pattern in the air and use your finger and thumb to pinch the fold every ½˝. The larger patterns may also be laid on a table and carefully folded.

tip Score the fold line first for fast, accurate folds. Line up a ruler on the fold line and use a seam ripper, awl, or butter knife to apply gentle pressure along the fold line.

Check the fold for accuracy. Turn the paper over and make sure the black fold line is visible from both sides of the fold. Adjust the fold if needed. When the fold is perfect, place the paper pattern on the table and crease the fold firmly with a fingernail or a wooden iron. Take enough time to fold very accurately. It will save headaches later.

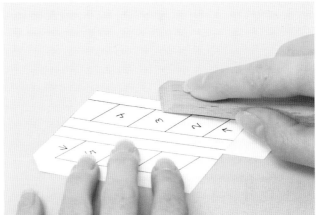
A wooden iron will firmly crease the fold.

Prepare the Star Fabrics

When purchasing fabric for the projects in this book, always buy extra to allow for cutting errors or remaking star points. Some of the projects require only a single 2˝ strip of fabric. Always buy enough fabric for one extra strip. The materials lists for the projects in this book provide for the extra strip.

1. Press the fabric and cut it to size using the Cutting Charts, pages 12–13. Don't be concerned about accuracy or grain lines. Fabric pieces cut smaller than suggested are difficult to place; slightly bigger is better. However, pieces cut too large get in the way, and it is too easy to sew in unwanted tucks and wrinkles. Use pieces no more than ½˝ larger than suggested and no more than ¼˝ smaller than suggested.

2. Stack the cut fabric pieces and assign color numbers to the fabric stacks. Use the layout diagrams in the project instructions to see where the color numbers will fall on the completed star. When assigning the color numbers to the fabric pieces, there are some things to keep in mind. The star tip should have high contrast with the background fabric. Choose a dark or busy fabric for the star center; it hides any mistakes in getting an exact match in the center.

3. Label the fabric stacks with the chosen color numbers. Do not skip this step thinking the numbers will be easy to remember; it can get confusing. Small, plastic ice-cream cups labeled with the number on the side are a good way to organize the fabric pieces. The plastic cups make it easy to grab the fabric number needed and place it close to the sewing machine. Zip-top bags or sticky notes also work well.

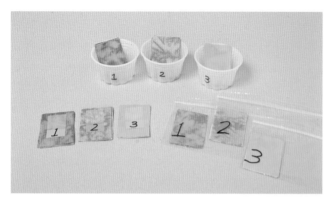

Use small, plastic cups, sticky notes, or zip-top bags to label star fabric pieces.

Cutting Charts

Use the cutting charts to cut the fabric pieces for the stars and the fabric for the background of the block as follows: (1) Find the chart for the number of rows in the pattern for your selected project. (2) In the first column,

Finished Patch Sizes, locate the desired size of the diamond patches, and refer to the corresponding row for the instructions that follow.

- **Diamond Patches column:** Provides the size (width × length) to cut the fabric pieces for the star. First, cut the star fabrics in strips the width of the first number. Then, cut these strips into rectangles the length of the second dimension listed.

- **List below the chart:** Provides the total number of fabric pieces to cut for each ring of the star.

- **Background Set-In Squares column:** Provides the size to cut the four small set-in squares for the background of the blocks. Cut the fabric in a strip the correct width, and then crosscut into four squares the stated dimensions.

- **Background Set-In Triangles column:** Provides the sizes to cut one large square of the background fabric to create the set-in triangles used to complete the block. Cut the large square on both diagonals to create four quarter-square triangles.

- **Square Up column:** Provides the size of the completed star block including seam allowances. Blocks will finish slightly larger. Square them up by carefully trimming.

 CUTTING CHART FOR 2-ROW STARS (3 sizes)
The 2 rows of the star create 3 concentric rings.

Finished Patch Sizes	Diamond Patches	Background Set-In Squares	Background Set-In Triangles	Square Up
	Cut * rectangular pieces for diamond patches.	Cut 4 small squares.	Cut large square, then cut into quarter-square triangles.	Trim completed star block to:
½″ diamond patches	1½″ × 1¼″	2″ × 2″	3½″ × 3½″	4″ × 4″
1″ diamond patches	2½″ × 1¾″	3″ × 3″	5″ × 5″	8″ × 8″
1¾″ diamond patches	2½″ × 4″	4½″ × 4½″	7″ × 7″	12½″ × 12½″

* Number of fabrics needed for each ring:

Ring 1, Star center: 8 pieces

Ring 2: 16 pieces

Ring 3, Star tips: 8 pieces

CUTTING CHART FOR 3-ROW STARS (3 sizes)

The 3 rows of the star create 5 concentric rings.

Finished Patch Sizes	Diamond Patches	Background Set-In Squares	Background Set-In Triangles	Square Up
	Cut * rectangular pieces for diamond patches.	Cut 4 small squares.	Cut large square, then cut into quarter-square triangles.	Trim completed star block to:
½″ diamond patches	1½″ × 1¼″	2½″ × 2½″	4″ × 4″	5½″ × 5½″
¾″ diamond patches	2″ × 1½″	3¼″ × 3¼″	5½″ × 5½″	8½″ × 8½″
1¾″ diamond patches	2½″ × 4″	7″ × 7″	11″ × 11″	19″ × 19″

Number of fabrics needed for each ring:

Ring 1, Star center: 8 pieces   **Ring 4:** 16 pieces

Ring 2: 16 pieces   **Ring 5, Star tips:** 8 pieces

Ring 3: 24 pieces

 CUTTING CHART FOR 5-ROW STARS (2 sizes)

The 5 rows of the star create 9 concentric rings.

Finished Patch Sizes	Diamond Patches	Background Set-In Squares	Background Set-In Triangles	Square Up
	Cut * rectangular pieces for diamond patches.	Cut 4 small squares.	Cut large square, then cut into quarter-square triangles.	Trim completed star block to:
½″ diamond patches	1½″ × 1¼″	3½″ × 3½″	5½″ × 5½″	9½″ × 9½″
¾″ diamond patches	2″ × 1½″	4¾″ × 4¾″	7½″ × 7½″	13½″ × 13½″

Number of fabrics needed for each ring:

Ring 1, Star center: 8 pieces   **Ring 6:** 32 pieces

Ring 2: 16 pieces   **Ring 7:** 24 pieces

Ring 3: 24 pieces   **Ring 8:** 16 pieces

Ring 4: 32 pieces   **Ring 9, Star tips:** 8 pieces

Ring 5: 40 pieces

Making Star Points

Assemble eight star points using the following instructions to paper piece the rows. Then join the rows together. The folded paper pattern does the work of matching points where the rows intersect.

Paper Piecing the Rows of the Star Point

Most paper-piecing patterns are sewn in number sequence. In this pattern, the numbers are *not* the order that the pieces are sewn. The numbers refer to the *color* of the fabric piece sewn to the corresponding number on the paper pattern.

The patterns are composed of the rows that make up a star point. Rows are pieced first and then sewn together to create a point. Piece the rows in alternating directions. This allows the seam allowances to nest together, which reduces bulk in the finished star. The arrows on the pattern indicate the direction for piecing in that particular row. Work in the direction of the arrow.

1. Start by orienting the pattern so that the row you will be working on has the arrow pointing to the right. In the diagrams and photos below, we use a 3-row star pattern and begin with the middle row. Use a small bit of fabric glue to attach the first fabric piece of the row to the unprinted side of the paper pattern. Hold the paper pattern up to a window or bright light to make sure the fabric piece completely covers the first diamond patch with at least ¼″ of excess fabric on all 4 sides of the diamond patch. Repeat for all 8 patterns, and place the paper patterns under something flat to dry for a couple minutes.

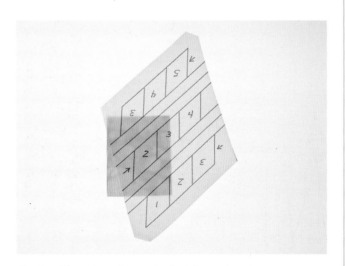

Glue first fabric piece of row to back of diamond patch on paper pattern.

Slip the patterns under a cutting mat to keep them flat while the glue sets.

2. Orient the paper pattern as described in the project instructions. Alternating rows are paper pieced with the paper pattern oriented one way. The paper pattern is then reoriented, and the remaining rows are paper pieced. By correctly orienting the pattern, the numbers on the row to be pieced will be right side up, making it much easier to place and piece the fabric.

3. Place the next piece of fabric in the row. Proper placement of this fabric piece seems to be the most difficult part of this process. To make it easier, hold the paper pattern up to a window or bright light, with the printed side toward you and the attached fabric on the back. Place the fabric piece, right sides together, behind the first diamond patch. Use the bottom right corner of the first diamond patch for placement.

The right corner of the first diamond patch is labeled *pin placement* on the placement diagram. Leave a ¼″ seam allowance on the bottom right corner and on the right-hand side of the diamond patch. All the extra fabric will be to the top and left when viewed from the side without the fabric attached. Check the placement diagram every time another fabric piece is added until you have mastered the process.

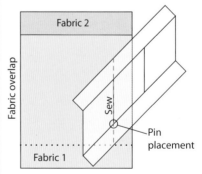

Use placement diagram to position fabric pieces as rows are paper pieced.

Hold the fabric piece in place, and slide the pattern and fabric into the machine. The paper pattern will be on the top, and the fabric will be against the feed dogs. Lower the needle, and then lower the presser foot.

✳ PIN PLACEMENT ✳

If the fabrics are very dark or the paper is hard to see through, stick any type of pin through the bottom right corner of the first diamond patch on the paper pattern. This point is labeled *pin placement* on the placement diagram. Then stick this same pin through the fabric piece ¼″ from the corner. Adjust the fabric so that it lies parallel to the right side of the first diamond patch, ¼″ away. Check the fabric against the placement diagram to ensure it is in the correct position. Leave the pin in the hole, and use it to pin the fabric in place.

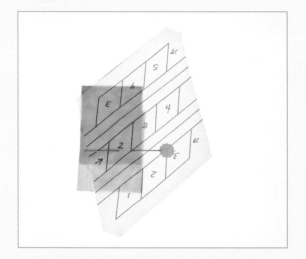

Position fabric piece and hold in place with a pin.

4. Sew exactly down the center of the solid sewing line between the diamond patches to attach the fabric piece. Do all the stitching from the printed side of the paper pattern. Use a short stitch length, 1–1.5. Start the seam ¼″ before the sewing line, and extend the seam ¼″ after the end of the sewing line.

To minimize tears in the paper, use a 1.5 stitch length when paper piecing on newsprint paper, vellum, and wash-away paper. Use a 1 stitch length on computer paper to make it easier to remove.

5. After attaching each fabric piece, always fold it over to check to see that the diamond patch is completely covered with fabric, with a ¼″ of extra fabric on all 4 sides of the diamond patch. If the diamond patch is not covered properly, then the stitching needs to be picked out, the fabric positioned correctly, and the diamond patch restitched.

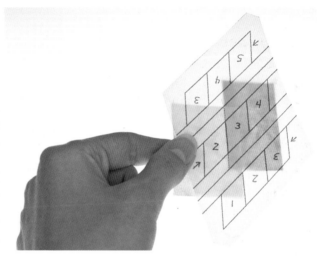

Hold pattern up to light to check proper placement of fabric.

6. Use small scissors to trim the seam allowance to a generous ⅛″ for the smaller stars. Trim to ¼″ for the larger stars.

Trim seam allowance to ⅛″.

7. Use a wooden iron, a craft stick, or a dry iron to press the fabric open.

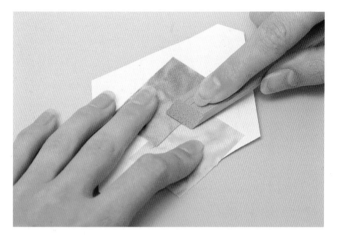

Press fabric open.

8. The 2-row stars, like those in *Tongan Star Dance*, page 37, have only 2 fabrics in each row. The row is now completed. For 3-row stars and 5-row stars, continue to add fabric pieces by repeating Steps 3–7 until the row is completed.

9. Use a dry iron to press the completed row. Use a small amount of fabric glue to hold the last fabric piece in the row to the paper pattern. The glue will keep the fabric down and out of the way while the remaining rows are paper pieced. Place the paper patterns under a mat to dry for a couple of minutes.

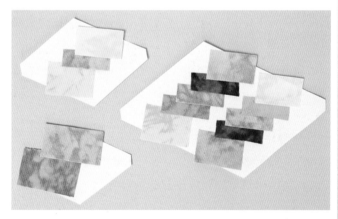

Complete first row or rows of 2-row star (bottom left), 3-row star (top left), and 5-row star (right). Glue last fabric piece of row to paper.

10. Once the technique for paper piecing the rows is mastered, it is much faster to piece multiple rows at once when making the 3-row star and the 5-row star. It saves time to piece all the rows with arrows pointing the same direction at the same time. Use the pin placement method described in Step 3, page 14, to place each fabric. Use the placement pin to hold the fabric pieces in place. Sew all the fabric pieces to the rows.

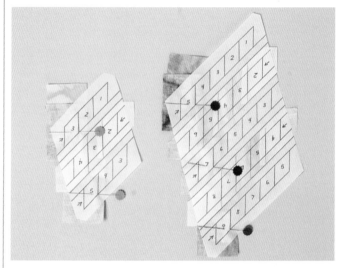

Pin fabric piece in place to multiple rows at once on the 3-row star (left) and 5-row star (right).

11. Trim the excess fabric away. Fold the paper pattern back on the fold line with the fabric on the outside. The excess fabric will be sticking up as little triangles beyond the fold line. Using a small pair of sharp scissors, hold them at an angle to the fold and cut the excess fabric off a little under the fold line. Be careful not to cut the paper pattern.

Trim excess fabric that sticks up in little triangles.

12. Open the paper pattern out flat again. A bit of the paper should show between the trimmed fabric and the fold line. Trim both sides of each pieced row. Do not trim the outside edges of the 2 outside rows. They are trimmed to size later.

13. Reorient the pattern as described in the project instructions to piece the remaining rows. Repeat Steps 1–12 to paper piece the remaining rows. After the rows are completed and trimmed, open the paper patterns out flat. Check for a ⅛″ gap of white paper showing between the trimmed rows. Carefully trim the fabric a little more if needed.

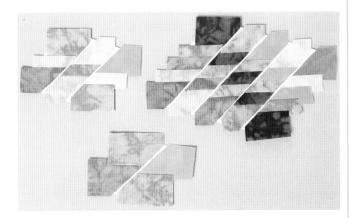

Completed 2-row star (bottom left), 3-row star (top left), and 5-row star (right). Notice ⅛″ gap of paper showing between completed, trimmed rows.

Join the Paper-Pieced Rows

This step is where the magic happens. The paper-pieced rows are joined together to form the star points, and the seams will match up perfectly.

1. Fold the paper pattern on the fold line with the fabric to the inside if making the 2-row star. For the 3-row star and the 5-row star, fold the paper pattern on any fold line with the fabric to the inside.

2. Starting at the edge of the paper pattern, sew *exactly* on the center of the seam line. Continue the seam to the edge of the paper pattern. The 8 paper patterns may be chain pieced to save time. Repeat to sew the remaining seam lines if making 3- or 5-row stars.

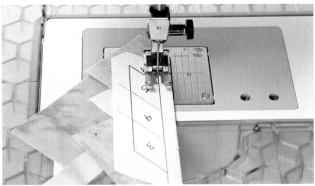

The seam to join paper-pieced rows starts at edge of paper pattern and follows exactly on center of seam line.

3. Open up the star point, and check for perfect alignment of the seams where the diamond patches intersect.

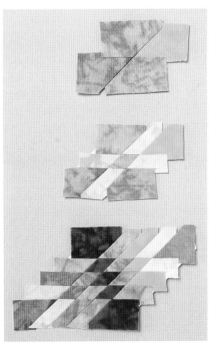

All intersections are perfectly aligned in star points for 2-row star (top), 3-row star (middle), and 5-row star (bottom).

4. See Troubleshooting Problem Stars, page 22, for help in correcting misaligned intersections.

Finish the Star Points

1. Press the completed star points. Use a hot iron, a spray bottle, or lots of steam, depending on the paper and ink used. See Tools and Supplies, page 4, for pressing hints for particular papers and inks. Press the seams toward patch #1 for 2-row stars, toward patch #5 for 3-row stars, and toward patch #9 for 5-row stars. Press until the 8 star points are very flat and dry.

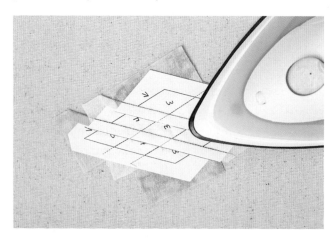

Use hot iron with steam to get star points very flat.

2. Use a ruler and rotary cutter to trim each star point, leaving enough extra fabric for an *exact* ¼″ seam allowance on all 4 sides of the paper pattern.

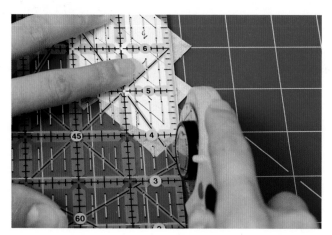

Trim completed star point.

3. Use small scissors to trim off the little seam allowance points. This is especially important in the small stars with ½″ patches. It removes some bulk and gives a better view of the seam line.

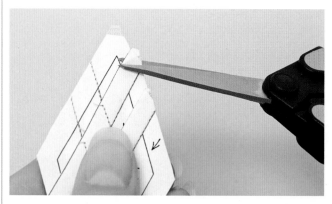

Trim seam allowance points with small, sharp scissors to give better view of seam line.

Assembling the Star

After the eight star points are pressed and trimmed, it is possible to arrange the star points with either the star tip or the star center at the center. Try both ways, and lay the star points on different backgrounds. Then pick a favorite orientation.

Two blocks made from same star points: one with dark purple fabric at center and one with dark purple at tips.

1. Join the star points in pairs. Use dressmaker pins (see Tools and Supplies, page 4, for recommendations on the best types of pins to use when matching intersections). Stick a pin through the back of the paper on the sewing line, and then through to the front of the next star point. Continue to add pins at each intersection of the diamonds.

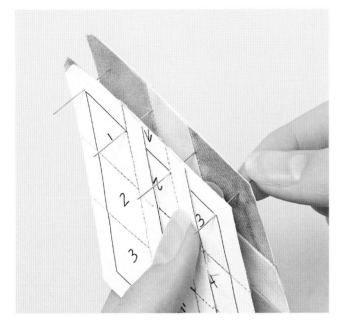

Use dressmaker pins to match each intersection.

2. Keeping the pins perpendicular to the paper star points, add 3 or 4 binding clips to hold the star points together, aligned and flat. Keep the pins perpendicular; do not lay them down and pin the star points together.

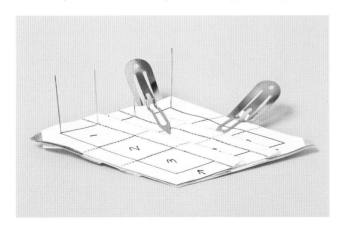

Use binding clips to keep star points aligned during stitching.

3. Remove the first pin, matching the star center, and lower the sewing machine needle into the hole that the pin made. Take 4 or 5 stitches and backstitch back to the pinhole. Do not stitch past the pinhole and into the seam allowance. Stitch slowly on the seam line, removing the pins and binding clips as the machine needle nears them. End on the pinhole at the inside corner with a few backstitches. Do not sew into the seam allowance. Repeat Steps 1–3 for the remaining 3 pairs of star points.

4. Join the pairs together using pins to match the intersections. Repeat Steps 2 and 3 to sew the pairs together.

5. Join the 2 halves of the star together using pins to match the intersections on only 1 side of the star. Repeat Steps 2 and 3 to sew the halves together on only that side of the center intersection. Sew from the star center out to the inside corner.

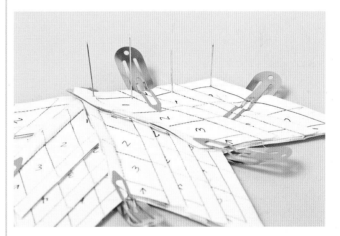

Pin, clip, and join halves of star together.

6. Use pins to match the intersections of the remaining seam of the star. Do not omit the pin matching the center of the star. Repeat Steps 2 and 3 to sew the last seam joining the star halves into a completed star shape. Refer to the Hand-Basting Method, page 23, if you are having problems matching the seams.

Adding a Background to Complete the Star Block

Background squares and quarter-square triangles are set into the spaces of the star to complete the star block. When the star points have been joined, it is possible to pin the star up on a design wall over different background fabrics. Select the background fabric that best enhances the fabrics in the star. The background pieces will not match up on the raw edges of the star block until the blocks are trimmed.

Cut and Mark Background

1. Choose a background fabric, and cut 4 small corner squares and a large square using the Cutting Charts, pages 12–13. To avoid stretching bias edges, don't make the diagonal cuts on the large background square until right before adding the quarter-square triangles to the star.

2. Line up the ¼″ line of a ruler with the edge of a background square. Use a mechanical pencil or fabric marker to make a short line ¼″ from the edge near one corner of the background square (mark on the wrong side of the fabric). Move the ruler to the next side, and repeat to make a small X at one corner of the background square. Repeat, marking the ¼″ seam lines on one corner of each of the background squares and on the inside corner of each of the 4 quarter-square triangles.

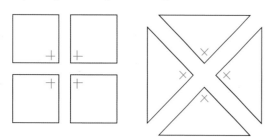

Mark ¼″ seam lines on wrong side of background pieces with fine point pencil or fabric marker.

Set-In Background Quarter-Square Triangles and Squares

Use the following instructions to set in the 4 quarter-square triangles to alternate spaces in the star. The seams are pressed, and then the background squares are set in to the remaining spaces of the star to create the corners of the block.

1. Place the fabrics right sides together. Then insert a dressmaker pin in the center of the X marked on a background triangle. Continue with the pin through the front of the star on an inside corner. Hold the pin perpendicular to the star, and add 1 or 2 binding clips to hold the pieces together. The outside edges of the star and the background will not match.

2. Sew the first seam with the background on the bottom and the paper on top. Sew on the seam line of the pattern, starting on the outside edge of the block and ending at the pinhole at the inside corner with a few backstitches. Do not sew into the seam allowance at the inside corner.

3. Match up the remaining edges of the star and the background triangle, and hold them together with a few binding clips. Use a binding clip to hold the star flat. Sew the remaining seam with the background fabric on top and the star on the bottom. Sew a ¼″ seam, starting at the outside edge and ending at the inside corner with a few backstitches.

Use binding clip to hold star flat while remaining seam adding background triangle is stitched.

4. Repeat Steps 1–3 to add each of the remaining quarter-square triangles. Press all the seams to the background.

A quarter-square triangle remains to be set in to star.

5. Set the background squares in to the remaining spaces of the star, using the procedure for setting in the quarter-square triangles in Steps 1–4. The outside edges of the background squares and triangles will not match up.

Completing the Block

1. Use fingers and tweezers to arrange the star seams in a spiral around the center. Hold in place, and then press the star thoroughly using steam.

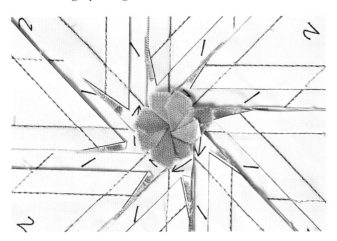

Star seams form spiral around center.

2. Press the outer seams toward the background.

3. Square up the completed star block to the size given in the Cutting Charts, pages 12–13, or in the project instructions. The finished sizes given in the cutting charts will leave extra background fabric around the star, making the star tips appear to float.

For star tips that do not float, square up the star block, leaving only ⅜″ of fabric beyond the star tips. The extra ⅛″ of background fabric will prevent the star tips from appearing to be cut off in the seam when they are sewn into the quilt.

4. Add borders to the star block, or use the completed star block in a quilt top. See Finishing the Quilt, page 25, for instructions to complete the quilt top. Do not remove the paper until the entire quilt is finished (see Removing the Glue and Paper, page 30).

Star Bright, Yvonne Oliphant, quilted by Debbie Myler, 2008.

Yvonne raided her stash while she was learning to make the paper fold-and-sew stars. The small and medium star blocks from *Tongan Star Dance* look great combined into a large quilt. Professionally quilted on a longarm machine by Debbie Myler.

Creating a perfect lone star is a challenge. This chapter describes some common errors encountered when making lone star blocks. Many of the mistakes can be fixed easily and quickly.

Diamond Patches Not Entirely Covered with Fabric

Open the star point after joining the rows together. Fabric may not entirely cover some patches. It is difficult to pick out all the seams and repair the problem. Discard the star point and make another one.

Some paper shows when diamond patch is not completely covered with fabric.

Prevent this from happening again by following these steps:

• Be sure to use the placement diagram, page 14, for adding every piece.

• Check for proper fabric placement after sewing each fabric piece. It is easy to pick out one seam and remove one piece of fabric if the placement is wrong. See the photo in Basic Instructions, Step 5, page 15, for checking fabric placement.

Don't worry if there is some paper showing at the *tips* of the star points after they are completed and trimmed. It does not matter if the whole seam allowance is covered with fabric. Hold the star point to the light and make sure there is at least a generous ⅛″ of fabric beyond the seam line.

A little extra paper showing at tip of star point is not a concern.

Intersections Between Patches Do Not Align

After stitching, open up the star point. Some of the intersections of the diamond patches may not align properly. If the folding was precise and the stitching was accurate, all the intersections should be close, and minor misalignments are not very hard to fix.

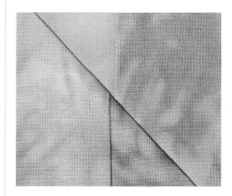

Improperly aligned intersections are evident in this star point.

• Pinch the seam allowance behind the mismatched intersection, and open the star to check. Does the alignment get better? If so, then increasing the seam allowance will correct the alignment. Only a very small adjustment will be required, so stitch just to the side of the previous seam, and check again for perfect alignment.

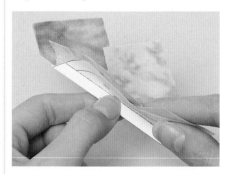

Pinch seam allowance and check fabric side to see if increasing it will correct mismatched intersection.

- If the seam is pinched and the alignment gets worse, then spread the seam apart to see if the alignment gets better. If the alignment improves, then pick out the stitching, and decrease the seam allowance.

Spread seam apart to see if alignment improves.

- Decrease or increase the seam allowance only where the intersections do not match. If all the intersections in a row need correcting, do not change the seam width at the beginning and ending of the seam. Changing the seam width at the edges of the star point will make it difficult to match the seams when the star points are joined.

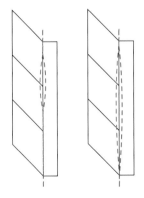

Seam is increased (red) and decreased (green) at only 1 intersection on left and for all intersections of row on right. Angle seam to seam line at both ends.

When using thicker fabrics or heavier-weight thread to make star points, test by completing one star point. Check the star point for correctly aligned seams, and make any needed adjustments. Make the same adjustments on the remaining seven star points, using the same thread and fabric. See Fabric, page 7, for more information on fabric choice and Tools and Supplies, page 4, for information on thread choice.

Center Does Not Match

Sometimes the star center does not match up easily. Carefully review all the steps and tips in Assembling the Star, page 18, and follow the steps below to solve the problem.

Hand-Basting Method

Hand basting before stitching the seams that join the star halves helps to get a good match in the star center. Basting is an easy way to get perfectly matched intersections without picking out and restitching any seam multiple times and ruining the paper. Baste any picked-out seam before stitching a second time. Basting will also help if the paper is slippery. Inexpensive, fuzzy polyester thread is great for basting. It grabs and holds well. Use a color different from the stitching thread so that it will be easy to see when removing.

1. Use pins first to match all the intersections and binding clips to hold the pieces aligned and together (see Steps 1 and 2 in Assembling the Star, page 19).

2. Do not knot the basting thread. Start with a stitch in the seam allowance to hold the thread, remove the first pin, and sew through the pinhole. Stitch a few more stitches in the seam allowance, and then sew through the next pinhole. End in the last pinhole. Do not knot the thread, but take a few stitches in the seam allowance to hold it firmly.

3. Baste the seam on each side of the center intersection with a separate piece of basting thread. Once you have basted both sides, check the star center for a perfect match. Make adjustments, and rebaste if necessary.

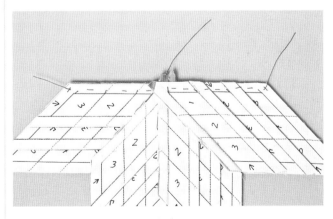

Baste seams joining star halves before sewing.

4. Sew both seams on the sewing machine. It may be easier to sew from the inside corner to the star center if the paper is bulky. Check the star center for a good match, and then remove the basting thread.

Other Tips for Improving the Center Match

- Never omit the pin matching the star center when stitching the last seam. The pin prevents the star points from shifting out of place.

- After basting the halves together, sew the seams from the inside corner to the star center.

- If the star center won't match no matter what, sew a button in the center. Use more buttons on the quilt, and make them part of the design.

A button at star center hides bad match.

Hole in the Center of the Completed Star

Sometimes a small hole may remain in the center of a star. Cut a small 1½″ circle of the same fabric used for the center diamonds of the star. Glue the fabric circle on the back of the star center, under the hole, before layering the quilt with batting and backing. Quilting the star will hold the circle of fabric in place permanently and prevent the batting from bearding through the hole.

Star Block is Not Flat

After all the background triangles and squares are set in, the star block may not lie flat. It can look like a hill or a bowl in the center.

Star block may not lie flat.

Usually this hill or bowl will go away when the paper is removed and the star block is pressed. If there is still excess fabric in the center of the star, quilt more heavily over the excess fabric. This will help the center to pull in, and the finished quilt should lie flat.

Paper Pattern Tears

The paper may tear on the stitching line. This often happens when a seam has been picked out. To correct this problem, use a washable glue stick to glue the previous fabric over the torn paper. Place it under a cutting mat to dry for five minutes or more before sewing on the next piece.

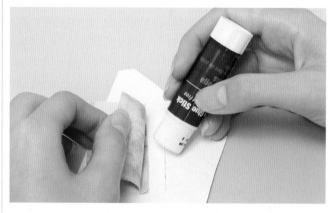

Stabilize paper tear by gluing fabric over tear.

Gluing the fabric over the tear also works if the paper tears while sewing the star points together. It is easy to tear the paper at the star center after picking out a seam. Gluing the fabric to the paper on the sewing line will give the paper more stability.

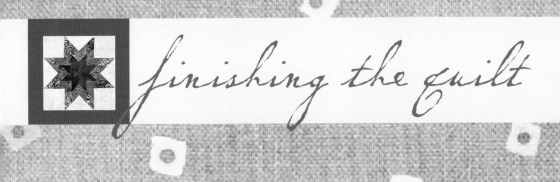

The star blocks are completed and the quilt top is assembled. Then the paper is removed so that the quilt top can be quilted and bound and a hanging sleeve and label added. The instructions for quilting, binding, and adding a small hanging sleeve provided in this chapter are adapted for the smaller projects in the book. For the larger quilts and wall hangings, use the finishing instructions in a quilter's reference guide such as *All About Quilting from A to Z*, available from C&T Publishing, to complete the quilt.

Borders

The projects in this book use five different borders. Mix and match the borders on any star block, or add them to other projects.

Solid Border

The solid border is used on *North Star*, page 34, for the outer border on *Prairie Star*, page 46, and the outer border on *Amish Star*, page 54.

1. Cut strips of fabric the desired width of the finished border plus ½˝ extra for seam allowances.

2. Measure the length of the quilt top through the center of the quilt. Cut 2 strips to this measurement. Sew the 2 strips to the sides of the quilt, using a ¼˝ seam. Press seams toward the border.

3. Measure the width of the quilt top through the center, including the attached border strips. Cut 2 strips to this measurement. Sew the strips to the top and bottom of the quilt. Press the seams toward the border.

Border with Corner Squares

The border with corner squares is used on *Spinning Sunshine*, page 50, and as the inner border on *Amish Star*, page 54.

1. Cut strips of fabric the desired width of the finished border plus ½˝ for seam allowances.

2. Measure the length of the quilt top through the center. Cut 2 strips to this measurement. Measure the width of the quilt top through the center. Cut 2 strips to this measurement.

> *tip* If the quilt top is square, measure both the length and the width through the center of the quilt top. If the two measurements are not exactly the same, use a measurement between the two numbers to cut the four strips. For example, if the length measures 16½˝ and the width measures 16˝, then cut 4 strips 16¼˝ long.

3. Sew 2 border strips to sides of quilt. Press the seams toward the border.

4. Cut 4 corner squares the width of the border strips. Sew the squares to both ends of the 2 remaining border strips. Press the seams toward the border strips.

5. Sew the borders strips with corner squares to the top and bottom of the quilt. Press the seams toward the border.

Scrappy Border

The scrappy border is used on *Bea's Star*, page 42, and on *Beggar's Star*, page 56. It is similar to the border with corner squares, but paper-pieced strips replace the solid fabric strips. The strips can be divided evenly, symmetrically, or irregularly.

Prepare Paper Patterns and Fabric

1. Use any paper suitable for paper piecing (see Tools and Supplies, page 4).

2. Cut strips of paper the desired width of the finished border plus ½″ for seam allowances.

3. Measure the width of the quilt top, and subtract ½″. Cut 2 paper strips to this measurement.

4. Measure the length of the quilt top, and subtract ½″. Cut 2 paper strips to this measurement. If the quilt is square, all 4 paper strips will be the same length.

 tip If the quilt top is bigger than the paper, join paper strips together with fabric glue to make the strips longer. Alternatively, use large sheets of regular newsprint paper.

5. Choose a border style, and fold the paper as instructed for the style below:

- **Regular Strips:** Create evenly sized sections by folding the paper strips in half lengthwise and then in half again. Continue to fold in half lengthwise to make 4, 8, or 16 even sections in the paper strips. See the top and right-hand borders in the photo at lower right. In this example, the top has 8 even sections, and the example on the right has 16 even sections.

- **Symmetrical Strips:** For sections that are not all the same size but are symmetrical for both ends, fold the paper in half first, and then fold in any chosen pattern. The bottom border in the photo shows an example of a border with symmetrical sections. The border on *Bea's Star*, page 42, is also folded this way.

- **Irregular Strips:** For a border with irregular sections, fold the paper in any chosen design. The left border in the photo was folded in irregular sections.

6. The fold lines are used as the sew lines. If the fold lines are hard to see, then trace over the folds with a pencil.

7. Cut fabric pieces at least ½″ wider and ½″ longer than the folded sections of the paper strips. Leftover fabric pieces from the star blocks may be the right size to piece the borders.

Paper Piece the Border Strips and Sew to Quilt

1. Attach a fabric piece to the back of the first section of the paper strip, using fabric glue. Leave a generous ¼″ of fabric extending beyond the end of the paper strip.

2. Paper piece the fabric onto the paper strips using the fold lines as sew lines. Press the fabric open after each piece.

3. Continue to add fabric pieces until the border strip is completed. Make sure there is a generous ¼″ of fabric extending beyond the end of the paper strip.

4. Press the completed border strip, and use fabric glue to hold the last fabric piece to the paper.

5. Use a ruler and rotary cutter to trim fabric that extends beyond the paper on the long sides of the border strips. Trim the ends of the border strips, leaving exactly ¼″ of fabric extending beyond the end of the paper.

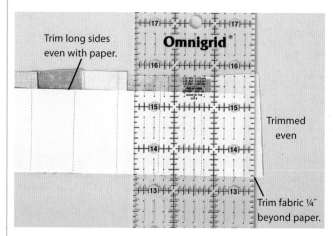

Trim sides of border strip evenly with paper edge. At both ends of border strip, ¼″ of fabric extends past paper.

6. Follow Steps 3–5 for Border with Corner Squares, page 25, to add the border to the quilt. Replace the plain border strips in the instructions with the paper-pieced border strips.

7. Remove the paper from the paper-pieced borders when removing the paper from the star.

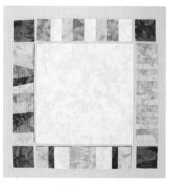

Paper-pieced border strips and corner squares are ready to sew to quilt. Clockwise from top: 8 even sections, 16 even sections, symmetrical around center, and irregular sections

Diamond Border

The inner border on *Prairie Star*, page 46, is a diamond border. This border uses the paper fold-and-sew technique for piecing diamond units and joining them together. The long string of diamond units is blocked and trimmed before it is added to the quilt.

Each finished diamond unit measures 1″ long. Use these directions to add the diamond border to any quilt finishing in a whole number. Diamond units at the corners will be chopped off if used on quilts with finished measurements at a fraction of an inch. Measure the quilt top to determine the number of 1″ diamond units needed for each side.

Prepare Patterns

1. Measure the length of the finished quilt top.

2. Calculate the number of diamond units needed for each side. Each diamond unit finishes to 1″ from point to point.

3. Make 4 copies of the diamond border *end* pattern, page 61.

4. Make 4 copies of the diamond border *end with cornerstone*, page 61.

5. Determine the number of *center* pattern strips to make the number of diamonds needed for each side. There are 7 diamond units in each border strip end pattern. If the border measurement is over 14″, make enough copies of the diamond border *center* pattern, page 49, to complete the border lengths needed.

6. Cut out the patterns on the cutting lines.

7. Lay out the pattern strips as they will be sewn on the quilt, with the center pattern(s) between the 2 end patterns on each side of the quilt top.

8. Count the number of diamond units needed for each side. Cut off any unneeded diamond units, using the fold line as the cut line. Cut diamonds only from the center unit or the interior ends of the end units. Do not cut off the diamonds at either end of the border.

9. Lay the patterns end to end, in order, for one side of the quilt, and use a pencil to number the diamonds consecutively. For example, a border with 21 diamonds will be numbered 1 to 21, from left to right, on the paper

pattern. This will help in sewing the pattern strips together in the correct order. Do this for all 4 border strips.

10. Fold the pattern strips carefully on all of the fold lines.

Border patterns are laid out, numbered, and folded on all fold lines.

Prepare the Fabric

1. Cut the fabric for the diamonds 1½″ × 1¼″. Cut enough for all the diamonds on all 4 sides of the quilt top.

2. Cut the background fabric 1½″ × 2″. Cut 2 background pieces for each diamond unit, plus 16 extra background pieces for the ends.

3. Cut 4 cornerstones 1½″ × 1½″ square.

Paper-Piece Borders

1. Glue a diamond fabric piece to the back of every other diamond on the pattern. Place the paper patterns under a cutting mat to dry for a few minutes.

2. Pin a background fabric to 1 side of each diamond fabric.

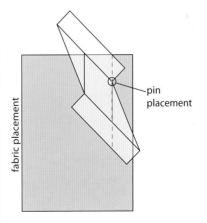

Placement diagram of background fabrics

3. Sew on all the backgrounds. Press.

4. Reorient the paper pattern with the opposite end up. Pin a background fabric to the remaining side of each diamond.

5. Sew on all the backgrounds. Press.

6. Use a small amount of fabric glue to hold the background fabrics to the paper. Dry under a cutting mat.

7. Fold the paper back on the fold lines, and trim the fabric that extends past the fold lines.

Trim excess fabric extending past fold lines.

8. Repeat Steps 1–7 to paper piece the remaining diamond units.

9. Finish paper piecing the ends by sewing background fabric pieces to all the shapes marked "B." Press.

10. Sew a 1½″ × 1½″ square to the pattern ends with a "C" square.

Diamond units are paper pieced and fabric trimmed. Notice ⅛″ gap of paper showing between diamond units.

11. Fold the paper patterns on the fold lines, and stitch all of the seams to join the diamond units on each strip.

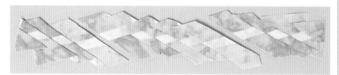

Diamond units are joined together by folding patterns and stitching seams.

Border Assembly

Piece all the diamond strips. Join the border strips together as indicated by the numbers marked on the diamonds.

1. Use dressmaker pins to match the intersections and binding clips to hold the strips together. Stitch on the seam lines.

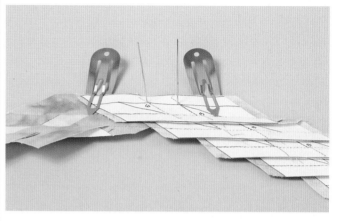

Join border strips together with pins and clips before stitching.

2. The completed border strips need to be blocked. To block the strips, measure the length, and adjust the strip until it is the correct length to fit the quilt. Pin to the surface of the ironing board. Use glass-head or flower-head pins to hold the borders in place. Use a ruler to keep the sides straight.

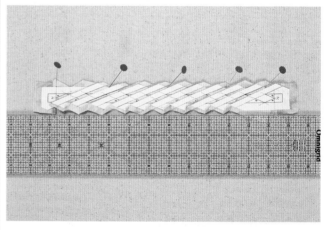

Use pins and ruler when blocking borders.

3. Iron to press the borders to the correct length, flat and straight, using the steam setting or a spray bottle with water. Leave the borders pinned until they are dry.

4. Use a rotary cutter to trim the edges of the borders, leaving a ¼″ seam allowance.

Trim edges of border, leaving ¼″ seam allowance.

Completed, pressed, and trimmed diamond border is ready to sew to quilt top.

5. Sew the 2 borders without cornerstones to opposite sides of the quilt top. Press.

6. Sew the 2 remaining diamond borders with cornerstones to the remaining sides of the quilt. Press.

7. Remove the paper from the diamond border when removing the paper from the rest of the quilt.

Star Points Border

The Star Points Border is on *Rainy Day Star,* page 57. Add it to any quilt top. Its construction is similar to mitering borders. Use any of the star point patterns in the book to complete the eight star points.

1. Prepare 8 star points following the directions in Basic Instructions, page 10. Press and trim the star points, but do not sew them into a star.

2. See the Cutting Chart for Star Points Border Strips, below. In the first column, find the star point pattern you are using. In the second column is the width to cut the border strips, and in the third column is the length.

3. Measure the unfinished block or quilt top (including the seam allowances). Cut the strips to the given width, and enough length to complete 4 quilt borders. Cut the border strips to the measured length *minus* the amount stated in the Length column of the chart. If the quilt top is square, the 4 border strips will be the same length. If the quilt is a rectangle, you will need to measure both the length and width of the top to determine the border lengths.

Cutting Chart for Star Points Border Strips

Star Point	Width to Cut Border Strip	Length to Cut Border Strip
2 row, ½″ patches	1¼″	Cut exact measured length.
2 row, 1″ patches	2″	Subtract ½″.
2 row, 1¾″ patches	3″	Subtract 1⅜″.
3 row, ½″ patches	1½″	Subtract ⅛″.
3 row, ¾″ patches	2⅛″	Subtract ⅝″.
3 row, 1¾″ patches	4¼″	Subtract 2⅜″.
5 row, ½″ patches	2¼″	Subtract ¾″.
5 row, ¾″ patches	3¼″	Subtract 1½″.

4. Fold the border strips in half, carefully matching the ends. Use a ruler with a 45° line to trim the ends of the border strips at a 45° angle.

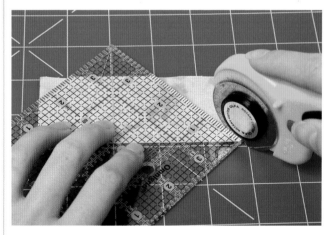

Trim ends of border strips at 45° angle.

5. Sew a star point to each end of the 4 border strips. Press the seam toward the border strip.

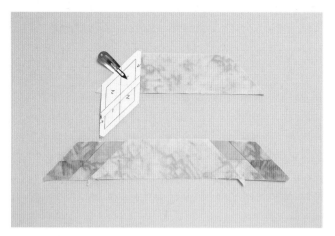

Border strip with star point ready for stitching and completed border strip.

6. Continue to construct the border in the same way you would a mitered border. Mark a ¼″ seam line on all 4 corners of the quilt top.

7. Match a border strip with a quilt edge.

8. Sew a few stitches, starting the seam at the marked ¼″ X. Take a few backstitches at the beginning and ending of each seam, but do not go into the ¼″ seam allowance.

9. Repeat to sew the 3 remaining border strips to the quilt top. Leave ¼″ of each corner free.

10. Sew the remaining diagonal seams, beginning and ending with a few backstitches.

11. Remove the paper from the star points in the border when removing the paper from the remainder of the quilt.

Removing the Glue and Paper

Assemble the entire quilt top, and then remove the pattern papers at the very end.

1. Release the fabric glue by immersing the finished quilt top in warm water for a few minutes if copy paper or computer printer paper was used. For newsprint paper or vellum, lightly spray the fabric side with water. Do not use water on wash-away paper. Make sure the ink used is water-fast before using water to release the glue. If the ink bleeds when wet, then do not wet the quilt top until removing all of the printed parts of the pattern. See Tools and Supplies, page 4, for more details about paper and ink.

2. Spread the quilt top on a towel to dry thoroughly. Don't try to remove the paper until the fabric and paper are completely dry. If the paper is still damp, it will shred into little pieces and be more difficult to remove.

3. Use fingers or tweezers to remove all the paper. Tweezers are useful to reach under the seam allowances and pull the paper out. Wash the quilt top again in warm water to remove any glue, paper shreds, or wash-away stabilizer remaining on the fabric.

Batting

Miniature and small quilts require thin batting. Thin polyester made for clothing or miniatures is a good choice. Thin, 100% cotton batting or 100% cotton flannel also works well in miniature quilts. Use white flannel to avoid any color or pattern showing through the quilt top, and preshrink the flannel to avoid puckers in the finished quilt. If the quilt is to be hand-quilted, test the flannel first by hand sewing some stitches. If the test stitches are too difficult, the flannel is too tightly woven, so choose another flannel with a looser weave.

Some batting can be very stiff in miniatures. It is a good idea to test the chosen batting first by stitching samples of the batting between muslin. Write on the muslin the type of batting inside. Machine and hand quilt the sample, and then wash to see how the batting shrinks. Save the quilted samples for later reference. A batting that might work well in one project will be the wrong choice in another.

Quilting

Thread choice is important in quilting miniatures. Regular-weight quilting thread will look like string on a miniature quilt. All aspects of a miniature quilt should be small in scale, even the thread.

For machine quilting, monofilament nylon thread works well to quilt in the ditch around the stars. For other machine quilting, try 60-weight cotton, fine silk, or fine-weight machine embroidery thread.

For hand quilting, 100-weight silk thread is wonderful. Silk thread slides out of a needle easily, so you will need to secure it in the needle. Follow the diagrams below. For hand quilting small quilts, 70-weight cotton thread is also available. Use small quilting needles, size 11 or 12, to achieve small stitches on little quilts.

To thread a hand-quilting needle with silk thread insert folded thread, pull folded end down over needle tip, and pull thread up so loop is caught around eye of needle. This will hold thread securely and prevent thread from slipping out of needle.

Use the fabrics in the quilt for inspiration when choosing quilting designs. Trace designs from fabrics or photos. Enlarge quilting designs, or use them just as they are. Shrink other quilting designs on a copy machine. On small reproduction quilts, traditional feathers and cables work well. Avoid hand quilting complicated designs on a miniature quilt. Complicated designs get lost and are hard to see.

Binding

Wash quilts with cotton batting designed to shrink before attaching the binding, or the quilt and binding may shrink at different rates, producing wavy or puckered edges. Machine or hand baste around the edge of the quilt after the quilting is finished. Wash the quilt in hot water, and dry to shrink the batting. Prewash fabrics used in bindings.

Narrow, Single-Fold ⅛″

Use a very narrow, ⅛″ single-fold binding with mitered corners on miniature quilts that are 15″ or smaller. (Use a regular ¼″ binding and refer to a general quilting book for the larger projects in this book.) When adding a ⅛″ binding, trim the quilt edge bigger than needed, and trim after sewing. This avoids stretching the quilt edge. Cut the binding wider than needed, and trim off extra. Wider fabric strips stretch less and are easier to handle.

1. Prepare the quilted quilt by basting around the quilt edge. Use a ruler and rotary cutter to trim the quilt edge, leaving a ¼″ seam allowance on all the sides.

2. Prepare the binding fabric. Cut cross-grain strips of binding fabric 1½″ wide. Use bias strips if the quilt edges curve or if the corners are rounded.

3. Join the strips together with diagonal seams to make a long strip the length of the perimeter of the quilt plus 8″.

4. Press the joining seams open. Fold the long binding strip in half lengthwise, wrong sides together, and press.

5. Start at the middle of one side of the quilt. Leave a 4″ tail of binding. Open the folded binding strip. Line up the single layer of binding ⅛″ in from the edge of the quilt. Hold the binding firmly without pulling it too tightly. Machine stitch the binding on the quilt, using a ¼″ seam allowance. The stitching will be ⅛″ from the edge of the binding and ¼″from the edge of the quilt.

6. At the corner of the quilt, stop sewing ¼″ away from the quilt edge, and take 3 or 4 backstitches. Remove the quilt from the machine. Fold the binding straight up away from the quilt, forming a 45° fold in the binding strip.

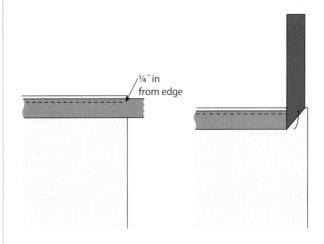

¼″ in from edge

7. Fold the binding strip down, keeping the top fold even with the raw edge of the previously sewn binding. Align the binding strip ⅛″ away from the next edge of the quilt. Start sewing ¼″ away from both edges of the quilt corner. Take a few stitches, 3 or 4 backstitches, and then continue sewing. The stitching will be ¼″ away from the quilt edge and ⅛″ away from the binding edge.

8. Repeat Steps 6 and 7 at each corner.

9. Sew the binding all the way around the quilt. Stop sewing 6″ from where the binding started.

10. Remove the quilt from the machine, and place it on a flat surface. Lay the binding tails along the gap, meeting them in the center of the gap. Fold one end of the binding down, toward the quilt, at a 45° angle. Use a pin to hold the binding strip in place. Fold the other end of the binding up, away from the quilt, at a 45° angle. Arrange the 2 binding folds to meet in the center of the gap. Crease the folds with a fingernail or wooden iron.

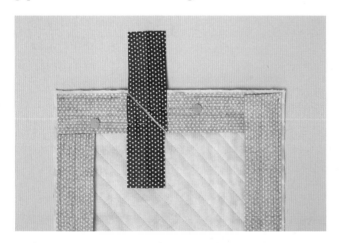

Binding strips meet in center of gap at 45° degree angle.

11. Pull the binding away from the quilt. Pin the 2 binding ends together, matching the creases. Sew the ends of the binding together by stitching on the crease line. Lay the quilt flat, and check that the binding is the correct length for the gap. If the binding does not lie flat, pick out the seam and try again.

12. When the binding lies flat, trim the extra fabric, leaving a ⅛″ seam allowance, and press it open. Finish sewing the binding on the quilt.

13. Use a ruler and rotary cutter to cut away ⅛″ of the quilt edge on all 4 sides. Use small scissors to cut away the excess width of the binding by cutting on the pressed fold.

14. Turn under ¼″ on the raw edge of the binding. Pull the turned-under edge of the binding to the back of the quilt, and pin it in place. Blindstitch the binding down, using a thread color that matches the binding fabric. Carefully arrange the miters in the corners with the sewing needle. Take a small stitch on both the front and back of the miter.

Hanging Sleeves

These instructions are for making little sleeves. They are the perfect size for quilts up to 15˝ wide that will hang on a wall.

1. Use leftover backing fabric to cut a strip 3½˝ wide. Measure the width of the finished quilt, and crosscut the strip to the length measured. Cut this strip in half.

2. Make a narrow hem on both ends of the 2 strips by folding under slightly less than ¼˝ and then folding under again, and sewing.

3. Fold both of the strips in half, right sides together, matching the raw edges. Use a ¼˝ seam to sew both into tubes. Start and end the seams with a few backstitches. Turn the tubes right side out, and press them with the seams to the back.

4. Place the 2 sleeves on the top of the quilt backing. Match the ends of the sleeves with the edges of the quilt, leaving a 1˝–1½˝ gap between the 2 sleeves. Pin the 2 sleeves in place.

5. Blindstitch the sleeves to the back of the quilt, stitching the sleeves only to the quilt backing so that the stitching does not show on the front of the quilt. Stitch down all edges of the sleeves, leaving the opening at each end of the tube free.

 tip When stitching the top edge of the sleeves, fold the sleeve down ¼˝ and pin it in place. Sew on this fold line. This creates a pucker of extra fabric in the sleeve for the dowel, without distorting the front of the quilt.

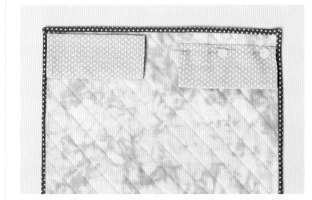
Fold top of sleeve down and blindstitch in place.

6. Slide a pencil, dowel, or chopstick into the sleeve, and use the center gap to hang over a hook or nail. A loop of string or wire slipped over the exposed dowel can hook over a nail on the wall.

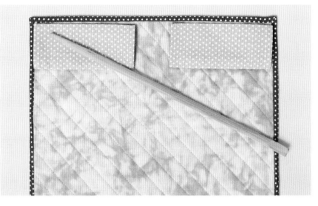
Slide chopstick into sleeve, and miniature quilt is ready to hang over hook or nail on wall.

Labels

Make a label for the back of the finished quilt. Use a fine-point permanent marker or embroidery to label the title of the quilt, the date, and your name on a piece of fabric. Include any other interesting information about the quilt on the label. Turn under the edges of the fabric label, and pin it to the back of the quilt. Blindstitch the label in place.

Little 2-row star point pattern from *Rainy Day Star*, page 57.

If the quilt is mailed or hung in a quilt show, then be sure to include an address, phone number, and email address on the label. This will help the quilt to be returned to you if any paperwork becomes detached.

north star

Finished 2-row star block size: 7½″ × 7½″

Finished quilt size: 10½″ × 10½″

The deep, rich colors of the batiks and hand-dyed fabric feel like a crisp, clear fall night with the stars so close that you can reach up and touch them. Batiks and hand-dyed fabrics are ideal for a first project. They are lightweight, they finger-press easily, and there is no wrong side of the fabric. This is the easiest star and a great project on which to learn the paper fold-and-sew technique!

Materials

Gold hand-dye: 1 large scrap at least 3″ × 18″ or ⅛ yard for star points

Multicolored batik: ¼ yard for star points and binding

Purple: ¼ yard for star and border

Light batik: ¼ yard for background

Backing: 1 square 14″ × 14″

Thin batting: 1 square 14″ × 14″

Cutting Instructions

Star and Background

Use the Cutting Chart, page 12, for the 2-row star with 1″ patches. Cut the fabrics for the star and the background.

Border

From the purple fabric, cut 1 strip 2″ × width of fabric.

Binding

From the binding fabric, cut 2 strips 1½″ × width of fabric.

Preparing Patterns and Fabric

1. Make 8 copies of the pattern for the 2-row star with 1″ diamond patches, page 36. Cut and fold the patterns (see Basic Instructions, page 10).

2. Check to ensure that there are enough star fabric pieces of each color for all the patches in each concentric ring. Label the fabric pieces with the number of the corresponding concentric ring.

Ring 1, star center: gold

Ring 2: multicolored batik

Ring 3, star tip: purple

tip Do not skip the labels on the star fabrics. It can get confusing.

Making 8 Star Points

1. Follow Steps 1–12 in Paper Piecing the Rows of the Star Point, pages 14–17, to paper piece the first row. Orient the pattern as shown to complete the first row.

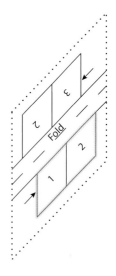

Pattern is oriented with #1 diamond patch down and #3 diamond patch up.

2. Reorient the pattern as shown to paper piece the second row. Follow Steps 1–13 in Paper Piecing the Rows of the Star Point, pages 14–17, to complete the second row.

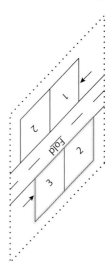

Pattern is oriented with #3 diamond patch down and #1 diamond patch up.

3. Complete the star points following the instructions in Join the Paper-Pieced Rows, page 17, and Finish the Star Points, page 18.

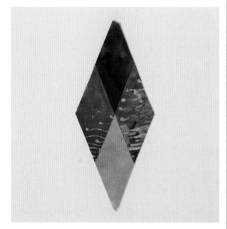

A completed star point for *North Star*

Completing the Star Block

Complete the star block by joining the 8 star points together and setting in the background triangles and squares.

1. Join the 8 completed star points together (see Assembling the Star, page 18).

2. Set in the background triangles and squares (see Adding a Background to Complete the Star Block, page 20).

Finishing

1. Press the block. Square up the completed star block to 8″ × 8″ (see Completing the Block, page 21).

2. Use the purple fabric to add a solid border (see Solid Border, page 25).

Layout and Assembly Diagram for *North Star*

3. Prepare the quilt top for finishing (see Removing the Glue and Paper, page 30).

4. Quilt, bind, and add a hanging sleeve and label (see Finishing the Quilt, page 25).

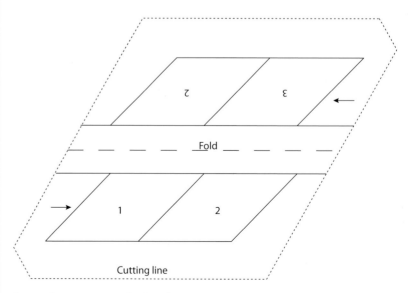

Pattern for 2-row star with 1″ patches

Finished 2-row star block sizes: 7½″ × 7½″, 12″ × 12″, and 41″ × 41″

Finished quilt size: 56″ × 56″

I had a lot of fun harmonizing my hand-dyed fabric with these beautiful Tongan batiks. The quilting designs were adapted from a book about Tongan flora to carry out the theme of lush tropical shadows. Combine the small 2-row star blocks made in the first project, *North Star*, page 34, with 4 medium-star blocks and one large center star to make this wall hanging. Look for fat quarters and other small cuts to get the variety of batiks and hand-dyed fabrics to make each of the small and medium stars different.

Materials

Assorted batiks and hand-dyed fabric: 1⅔ yards total for small and medium stars

Orange/fuchsia batik: ½ yard for large star

Dark blue hand-dyed fabric: ⅔ yard for large star

Blue/black batik: ½ yard for large star

Yellow batik: 1½ yards for background

Yellow/black batik: 1¼ yards for borders

Red batik: ½ yard for binding

Backing: 3⅔ yards

Batting: 1 square 64″ × 64″

Cutting Instructions

Make the small and medium stars from assorted batiks and hand-dyed fabric. For each star block, choose 3 coordinating fabrics for the star points. Use the same yellow batik for the background squares and triangles in all of the star blocks.

Small Stars

Make 32 copies of the pattern for the 2-row star with 1″ diamond patches, page 36. Cut and fold the patterns (see Basic Instructions, page 10). Use the Cutting Chart, page 12, for the 2-row star with 1″ diamond patches. Cut enough fabric for 4 stars. The yellow batik is the background.

Medium Stars

Make 32 copies of the pattern for the 2-row star with 1¾″ diamond patches, page 41. Cut and fold the patterns (see Basic Instructions, page 10). Use the Cutting Chart, page 12, for the 2-row star with 1¾″ diamond patches. Cut enough fabric for 4 stars. The yellow batik is the background.

Large Star

Star Points

1. Enlarge the large diamond template, page 41, to 200% and make 1 copy using any type of paper or template material. Mark the grain line on the template.

2. Cut the blue hand-dyed fabric into 4 strips 4¾″ × width of fabric. Cut the orange/fuchsia batik and the blue/black batik into 2 strips 4¾″ × width of fabric.

3. Open the cut fabric strips to 1 layer. Stack the 4 strips of blue hand-dyed fabric together, carefully matching the ends and edges. Open the orange/fuchsia batik and the blue/black batik strips, and stack all 4 of the batik strips together.

4. Place the large diamond template faceup on the stacked blue hand-dyed fabric strips. Match the marked grain line on the template with the crosswise grain of the fabric. Use a large ruler with a 45° line to cut off the end of the stack of fabric strips at a 45° angle. Use the ruler and the large diamond template to cut the remainder of the stack of blue hand-dyed fabric strips into 16 large diamonds.

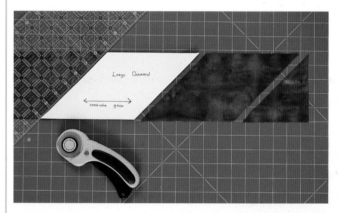

Use large diamond template and ruler with clearly marked 45° line to cut stacked fabric strips into large diamonds.

5. Turn the template over, and place the large diamond template facedown on the stacked batik strips. Repeat the cutting for the stacked batik strips. Cut 8 diamonds from each batik fabric.

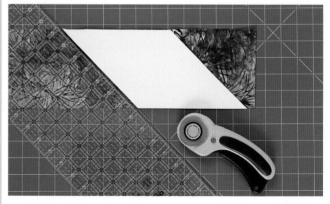

Turn the template over for the second stack of strips so that the grain line will fall on a different side of the diamond.

Background

1. Cut 1 square 18¼″ × 18¼″ out of the yellow batik.

2. Fold the square in half diagonally. Make sure the edges are even, and gently press the fold.

3. Fold the resulting triangle in half on the other diagonal. Match the edges carefully, and press both folds with a hot iron.

4. Line up the edge of a long ruler along 1 fold line with only ¹⁄₁₆″ of folded edge showing beyond the ruler. Do not try to measure the ¹⁄₁₆″. Just approximate a very small amount beyond the ruler edge. Use a rotary cutter to trim ¹⁄₁₆″ from the folded edge. Repeat to trim ¹⁄₁₆″ off the other fold line. This procedure will make 4 large quarter-square triangles.

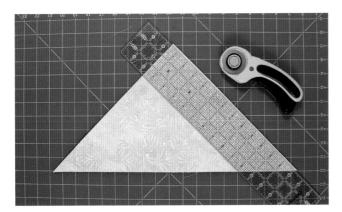

Large background square is folded on both diagonals to create a triangle, and ¹⁄₁₆″ is trimmed from both folded edges.

Borders

Cut 4 strips 8″ × length of fabric.

Binding

Cut 6 strips 2¼″ × width of fabric.

Assembly

Make the large center star from large diamonds, background triangles, and 4 medium star blocks. Use the 4 small star blocks as corner squares in the border.

Small Stars

Make 4 small star blocks using the instructions for *North Star*, page 34. Square up the 4 completed small star blocks to 8″ × 8″. Set these aside to use as corner blocks in the border.

Medium Stars

Make the medium stars using the same instructions used for the small stars in *North Star*, page 34, and the pattern for a 2-row star made from 1¾″ diamond patches, page 41. Make 4 medium star blocks. Square up the completed blocks to 12½″ × 12½″.

Large Star

Star Points

1. Stack the large diamonds in 3 stacks with the like-colored diamonds together in the same stack. Divide the hand-dyed blue stack into 2 stacks of 8 diamonds each. Arrange the stacks into a diamond four-patch as shown.

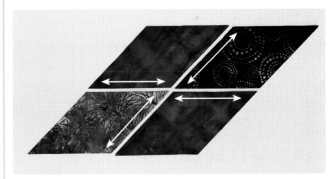

Arrange the stacks, placing the straight of grain of each diamond as indicated by the arrows.

2. Sew the diamonds into pairs by stitching a blue diamond to an orange/fuchsia diamond, and a blue/black diamond to a blue diamond. Repeat for all the stacked diamonds. Keep the bias edges on the bottom toward the feed dogs when stitching the seam to minimize stretching. Press the seams toward the straight of grain.

3. Sew the rows together to complete the four-patch, matching the seam at the ¼″ seam line and not at the edge of the fabric. Press the seam toward the orange/blue row. Repeat for all 8 star points.

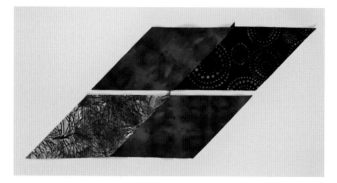

Join large diamonds in rows to complete a star point of the large center star.

Star Assembly

1. Use a pencil or fabric marking pen to mark ¼˝ seam lines with a small X at all 4 points of each large star point (see Cut and Mark Background, page 20).

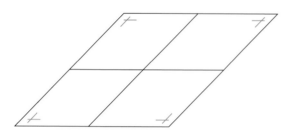

Mark the diamond points.

2. Assemble the large star using the same procedure used when joining the star points in the smaller stars (see Assembling the Star, page 18). Use pins to match the marked X's, and use pins rather than clips to hold the star points together.

3. Join the large star points in pairs. Start stitching at the X marked at the star center, and end the seam at the X marked on the inside corners of the star points. Backstitch at each end, but do not stitch into the seam allowances.

4. Join the pairs of star points into halves, repeating directions in Step 2.

5. Join the 2 halves of the star together with 2 separate seams. Start the seams at the star center, and end the seams at the X marked at the inside corners with a few backstitches. Handle the star points very carefully to avoid stretching the bias edges. Do not press the seams now.

Add Large Star Background

1. Mark the backgrounds (see Cut and Mark Background, page 20). Mark ¼˝ seam lines with an X on the inside corners of the 4 quarter-square triangles cut from the large 18¼˝ × 18¼˝ background square. Mark the ¼˝ seam lines on 1 corner of all 4 medium star blocks.

2. Sew the large quarter-square triangles and medium star blocks to the large star (see Set-In Background Quarter-Square Triangles and Squares, page 20). This time, the outside edges of the background and the star should match perfectly.

3. Press the completed large star by arranging the seams of the large star into a spiral around the star center. See the photo on page 21.

Border

Add a border with corner squares (see Border with Corner Squares, page 25). Use the small star blocks for the corner squares of the border.

Layout and Assembly Diagram for *Tongan Star Dance*

Finishing

1. Prepare the quilt top for finishing (see Removing the Glue and Paper, page 30).

2. Complete the quilt (see Finishing the Quilt, pages 30–32). This quilt uses a binding wider than ⅛˝. Consult a quilter's reference guide like *All About Quilting from A to Z* for a different size of binding. *Tongan Star Dance* was stitched in the ditch around the stars with clear nylon monofilament thread. The large star and backgrounds were quilted with tropical foliage designs.

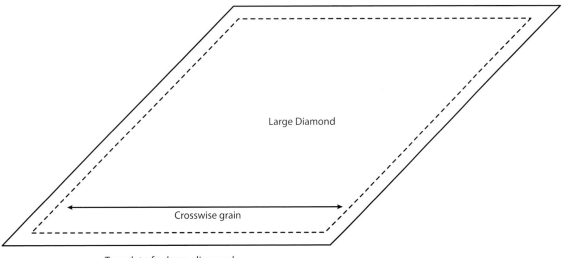

Large Diamond

Crosswise grain

Template for large diamond

Enlarge 200%.

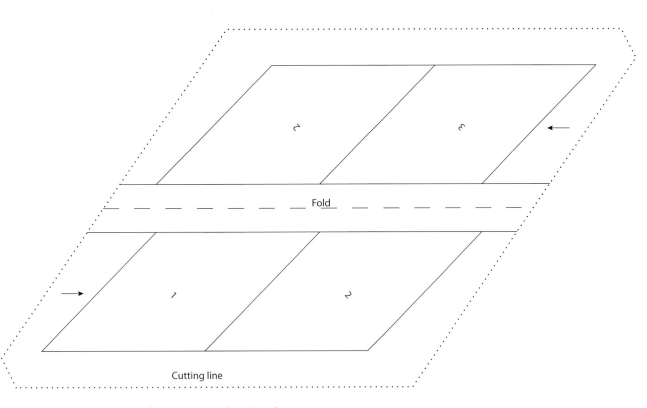

Fold

Cutting line

Pattern for 2-row star with 1¾″ patches

 *bea's star*

Finished 3-row star block size: 8″ × 8″

Finished quilt size: 11″ × 11″

I loved the black prints in this collection of '20s reproductions. Working with the fabric colors and prints my grandma and great-grandma would have had in their sewing baskets evokes the feeling of being in another era and stitching side by side with them. The completed quilt reminded me of a photo of my Grandma Bea all dressed up to go out on the town, so I named it after her. This is a great project on which to learn the fold-and-sew technique for those familiar with paper piecing. The *Bea's Star* block has 3 rows rather than the 2 rows used to make the first project. I made my star scrappy by combining more than one print in some of the concentric rings.

Materials

Assorted turquoise/blue prints: ⅛ yard total for star points and border

Assorted dark prints: ⅛ yard total for star points

Black solid: ⅛ yard for star points

Red print: ⅛ yard for star points

Red solid: Large scrap at least 2½″ × 15″ or ⅛ yard for star points

Light black print: ¼ yard for background

Turquoise solid: Large scrap at least 6″ × 6″ for border corner squares

Black print: ⅛ yard for border

Red plaid: ⅛ yard for binding

Backing: 1 square 15″ × 15″

Batting: 1 square 15″ × 15″

Cutting Instructions

Star and Backgrounds

Use the Cutting Chart, page 13, for the 3-row star with ¾″ patches to cut the fabrics for the star and the background.

Border

1. From the black print, cut 4 rectangles 2½″ × 6¾″.

2. From the turquoise print, cut 8 rectangles 2½″ × 1¾″.

3. From the turquoise solid, cut 4 squares 2″ × 2″ for the corner squares.

Binding

From the red plaid, cut 2 strips 1½″ × width of fabric.

Preparing Patterns and Fabric

1. Make 8 copies of the pattern for the 3-row star with ¾″ diamond patches, page 45. Cut and fold the patterns (see Basic Instructions, page 10).

2. Use the Cutting Chart, page 13, for the 3-row star, to determine the correct number of fabric pieces needed for each concentric ring. Label the fabric pieces with the number of the corresponding concentric ring.

Ring 1, star center: turquoise/blue prints

Ring 2: dark prints

Ring 3: black solid

Ring 4: red prints

Ring 5, star tip: red solid

 Combine two or three different fabrics in the same concentric ring for a scrappy look. Make sure the prints have similar colors and values so they will all look the same when viewed from a distance.

Making 8 Star Points

1. Follow Steps 1–12 in Paper Piecing the Rows of the Star Point, pages 14–17, to paper piece the middle row. Orient the pattern as shown to complete the middle row.

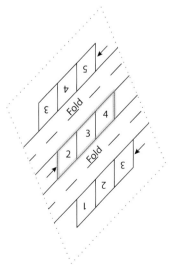

Paper piece middle row with diamond patch #1 down and diamond patch #5 up.

2. Reorient the pattern as shown, and then paper piece the remaining 2 rows. Follow Steps 1–13 in Paper Piecing the Rows of the Star Point, pages 14–17.

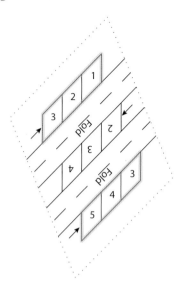

Paper piece 2 remaining rows with #5 diamond patch down and #1 diamond patch up.

 Piece the two remaining rows at once to save time. Use the pin placement method, page 15, to place the fabrics, and then sew them in place.

3. Complete the star points (see Join the Paper-Pieced Rows, page 17, and Finish the Star Points, page 18).

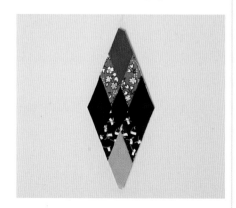

A completed star point for *Bea's Star*

Completing the Star Block

1. Join the 8 completed star points together (see Assembling the Star, page 18).

2. Set in the background triangles and squares (see Adding a Background to Complete the Star Block, page 20).

Finishing

1. Press the block. Square up the completed star block to 8½″ × 8½″ (see Completing the Star Block, page 21).

2. To make the scrappy border, cut 4 paper strips 8″ × 2″. Fold the strips in half. Fold in each end approximately 1″. Use the folded paper strips, dark print, turquoise print, and turquoise solid cornerstones to assemble a scrappy border. The dark print and turquoise print pieces are cut oversize to allow easier placement when paper piecing (see Scrappy Border, page 25).

Layout and Assembly Diagram for *Bea's Star*

3. Prepare the quilt top for finishing (see Removing the Glue and Paper, page 30).

4. Quilt, bind, and add a hanging sleeve and label (see Finishing the Quilt, page 25). I machine quilted the star in the ditch and hand quilted the background and border using motifs from the fabric.

I have included a pattern for a larger-size, 3-row star, for quilters who would like to try the paper fold-and-sew technique but do not want to try a miniature. The instructions for the larger star, which measures 18½″ × 18½″, are the same as for *Bea's Star*. Use the pattern for a 3-row star made from 1¾″ diamond patches, page 62, and the Cutting Chart, page 13, for the 3-row star made from 1¾″ diamond patches to prepare the fabrics. The quilt *Charming Garden*, page 9, is made from this pattern.

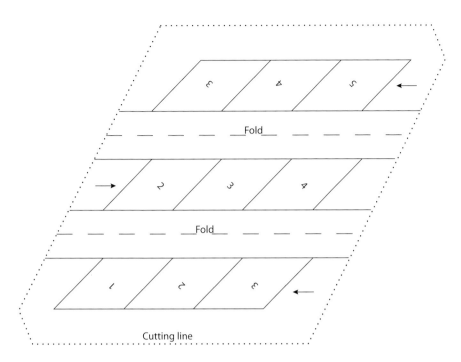

Pattern for 3-row star with ¾″ patches

Bride's Star, Lorraine Olsen, 2008.

One star block looks beautiful framed on the wall. *Bride's Star* is made with 1″ wide grosgrain ribbon instead of fabric using the pattern for a 3-row star with ¾″ patches. Eight fussy cut background squares were set into the background of the star. The paper was left in when the star was framed.

prairie star

Finished 3-row star block size: 5″ × 5″

Finished quilt size: 27″ × 27″

There are many examples of the Prairie Star pattern used in full-size quilts from the nineteenth century. Two of the concentric rings in the Prairie Star block use the same fabric as the block background. This makes the tips and rings of the stars appear to float on the quilt. Make a miniature version of a classic pattern by using Civil War–era reproductions with tan print backgrounds. The star blocks in this wall hanging are the same as in the *Bea's Star*, page 42, only using smaller, ½″ diamond patches. The blocks are set on point and surrounded with a pieced diamond border. The tiny patches and narrow border make this miniature a challenging project.

Materials

Assorted dark reproduction prints in blue, red, gold, and brown: ⅔ yard total for star points

Assorted tan prints: 1⅛ yards total for stars, backgrounds, setting squares, setting triangles, and diamond border

Assorted brown prints: ¼ yard total for diamond border

Red print: Large scrap at least 1½″ × 8″ for cornerstones in border

Dark tan print: ⅞ yard for diamond and outer borders

Gold print: ¼ yard for binding

Backing: 1 yard

Batting: 1 square 33″ × 33″

Cutting Instructions

Star Blocks

Use the Cutting Chart, page 13, for the 3-row star with ½″ diamond patches to cut the fabrics for the star and the background. Cut enough fabric pieces for 9 star blocks. Use the dark reproduction prints for the star points. Use the tan print for the #2 and #4 concentric rings of the star block. Use the same tan prints as the background for each block.

Setting Squares and Triangles

From the tan prints, cut:

4 squares 5½″ × 5½″ for setting squares

2 squares 8¼″ × 8¼″, and then cut the 8¼″ squares on both diagonals to make 8 quarter-square setting triangles

2 squares 4⅜″ × 4⅜″, and then cut the 4⅜″ squares on 1 diagonal to make 4 half-square triangles for the corners

Diamond Border

1. From the brown prints, cut 3 strips 1½″ × width of fabric. Cut the strips into 84 rectangles 1½″ × 1¼″.

2. From the dark tan prints, cut 5 strips 1½″ × width of fabric. Cut the strips into 88 rectangles 1½″ × 2″.

3. From the tan prints, cut 5 strips 1½″ × width of fabric. Cut the strips into 88 rectangles 1½″ × 2″.

4. From the red print, cut 4 squares 1½″ × 1½″.

Outer Border

From the dark tan print, cut 6 strips 3″ × width of fabric.

Binding

From the gold print, cut 3 strips 1½″ × width of fabric.

Making 9 Star Blocks

1. Make 72 copies of the pattern for a 3-row star with ½″ diamond patches, page 49. Cut and fold the patterns (see Basic Instructions, page 10).

2. Prepare the star fabrics using the Cutting Chart, page 13, for the 3-row star, to determine the correct number of fabric pieces needed for each concentric ring. Label the cut fabric pieces with the number of the corresponding concentric ring. Use the same fabric for the block background and the #2 and #4 concentric rings.

Ring 1, star center: dark print

Ring 2: background fabric

Ring 3: dark print

Ring 4: background fabric

Ring 5, star tip: dark print

3. Complete 1 star block using the instructions for the *Bea's Star* block, page 43, (see Making Star Points, page 14, and Completing the Block, page 21). Repeat to make 9 star blocks total.

Completed star point for *Prairie Star*, with #2 and #4 concentric rings using same fabrics as background of block.

4. Square up the 9 completed star blocks to 5½″ × 5½.″

Joining the Blocks

1. Use the Layout and Assembly Diagram for *Prairie Star* to arrange the star blocks, setting squares, setting triangles, and corner triangles.

2. Sew the blocks, setting squares, and setting triangles into diagonal rows. Sew the rows together. Press toward the setting squares and triangles.

3. Add the corner triangles. Press toward the corner triangles.

Borders

Diamond Border

Refer to Diamond Border, page 27, for instructions; the illustrations show shorter patterns for easier visibility. Each side of the *Prairie Star* quilt has 21 diamond units.

1. Make 4 copies each of the center, end, and end with cornerstones patterns, pages 49 and 61. Cut them out on the cutting lines.

2. Lay out all 12 patterns as they will appear on the sewn quilt, with 2 opposite sides of the quilt having 2 end patterns and a center pattern, and the other 2 sides having 2 end with cornerstones patterns and a center pattern.

3. Number the diamonds 1–21 for each side of the quilt. The numbers will make it easier to assemble the border pattern pieces in the correct order later.

4. Mark the patterns with outside and inside edges for the 2 different background colors. The inside edge will use the tan prints, and the outside edge will use the dark tan prints.

5. Fold all the border patterns (see Fold Copies of Star Points Pattern, page 11). Paper piece using the brown fabric for the diamonds, the tan and dark tan prints for the backgrounds, and the red print squares for the cornerstones.

6. Join the strips together, using the numbers to assemble the border patterns in the correct order.

7. Measure the quilt top through the center. Use this measurement when pinning the diamond borders to the ironing board. Block, steam, and trim the 4 pieced diamond borders.

8. Sew the 2 borders without cornerstones to opposite sides of the quilt. Press seam toward the quilt. Sew the 2 borders with cornerstones to the remaining sides of the quilt. Press.

Outer Border

Use the 3″ strips of dark tan print to add a solid border (see Solid Border, page 25).

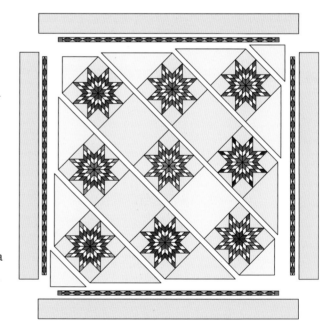

Layout and Assembly Diagram for *Prairie Star*

Finishing

1. Remove the paper from the star blocks and the diamond border (see Removing the Glue and Paper, page 30). Press the completed quilt top.

2. Quilt, bind, and add a hanging sleeve and label (see Finishing the Quilt, page 25). *Prairie Star* is machine quilted in the ditch around the stars. The setting squares and setting triangles are hand quilted with feathered designs. The outer border is quilted in a cable design.

Pattern for 3-row star with ½″ patches

Pattern for center diamond border

 *spinning sunshine*

Finished 3-row star with pieced corners block size: 8″ × 8″

Finished quilt size: 24¾″ × 24¾″

Bright, complementary colors combined with black prints give a lot of energy to the starburst design. The block is not as difficult as it appears. The solid background of *Bea's Star*, page 42, is replaced by paper-pieced sections. This gives a wonderful starburst effect to the 3-row star block. A single starburst block would also make a delightful little quilt. This quilt provides an opportunity to use many bright scraps and hand-dyed fabrics.

Materials

Assorted bright prints and solids, black prints, and white prints: 1¼ yards total for star points and starburst corner triangles

Black solid: 1 yard for background, cornerstones, and binding

Assorted bright tone-on-tones: ¼ yard total for sashing

Black-and-white print: ¼ yard for border

Red-orange tone-on-tone: Large scrap at least 4″ × 13″ or ⅛ yard for corner squares

Backing: 1 yard

Batting: 1 square 31″ × 31″

Cutting Instructions

Starburst Blocks

1. Use the Cutting Chart, page 13, for the 3-row star with ¾″ patches to cut the fabric for each star. Cut enough fabrics for 4 stars. Do *not* cut the backgrounds using the cutting chart. For the starburst block, replace the plain background squares and tri-angles with pieced corner sections.

 Cut the star fabric in strips, and arrange the strips on a design wall to plan the colors of each starburst block. Strive for high contrast of color or value between the concentric rings to achieve the energy of *Spinning Sunshine*.

2. For the pieced starburst corner sections of each starburst block, use the same color as the star's #4 and #5 fabrics as follows:

> From the #4 fabric of each star, cut 1 strip 1½″ × width of fabric. Cut the strip into 8 squares 1½″ × 1½″.
>
> From the #5 fabric of each star, cut 1 strip 1½″ × width of fabric. Cut the strip into 16 squares 1½″ × 1½″.

3. Cut the solid black fabric for the backgrounds of all the stars as follows:

> Cut 3 strips 3½″ × width of fabric. Cut the strips into 24 squares 3½″ × 3½″. Cut the squares on both diagonals to yield 96 quarter-square triangles.
>
> Cut 2 strips 4½″ × width of fabric. Cut 8 squares 4½″ × 4½″. Cut these squares on 1 diagonal to yield 16 half-square triangles.

Sashing and Cornerstones

1. From the assorted bright tone-on-tones, cut 12 rectangles 1¾″ × 8½″ for sashing.

2. From the solid black, cut 9 squares 1¾″ × 1¾″ for the cornerstones.

Border

1. From the black-and-white print, cut 2 strips 3″ × width of fabric.

2. From the red solid, cut 4 squares 3″ × 3″ for the corner squares.

Binding

From the black solid, cut 3 strips 2″ × width of fabric.

Making Starburst Blocks

Star

1. Use the pattern and instructions for the *Bea's Star* block, page 43, to make a star. Complete the steps in Preparing Patterns and Fabric, page 11, and Making Star Points, page 14.

2. Join the 8 completed star points using the instructions in Completing the Block, page 21. Do not set in background squares or triangles. Repeat to make 4 stars total.

Starburst Corner Triangles and Squares

Prepare Patterns and Fabric

1. Make 32 copies of the starburst corner pattern, page 60. Cut out the patterns on the cutting lines. Carefully fold on all of the fold lines.

2. Use the same #4 and #5 for the starburst corners as used when making each star. Label the fabrics.

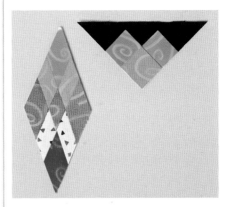

Notice that #4 fabric and #5 fabric are same for completed star point and completed starburst corner triangle.

Starburst Corner Assembly

First Row

1. Start at the arrow by the #4. Glue a #4 fabric piece to the back of the #4 square on the paper pattern. Dry for a couple minutes.

2. Place a #5 fabric on the #4 fabric, right sides together. Sew on the sew line to attach the #5 fabric. Trim the seam, and press.

3. Sew on a black background quarter-square triangle to complete the row. Press, and glue down the background triangle.

4. Fold back the paper pattern on the fold line, and trim the fabric that extends past the fold line.

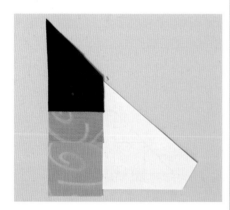

First row of starburst corner pattern is pieced, pressed, and trimmed.

Remaining Row

1. Start at the arrow end of the remaining row on the corner pattern, and glue down a background piece to the "B" triangle on the paper pattern.

2. Sew on a #5 fabric piece. Press.

3. Sew on a background fabric triangle to the #5 fabric square. Press, and glue down the background triangle.

4. Fold the paper pattern back on the fold line, and trim all the fabric that extends past the fold line.

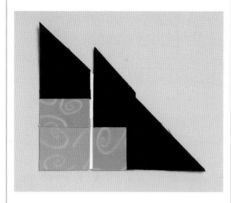

All rows of starburst corner are pieced, pressed, and trimmed.

Joining Rows

1. Fold the paper pattern on the fold line with the fabric to the inside. Sew on the seam line. Start stitching at the edge of the fabric, and stitch to the edge of the fabric. Repeat for all 8 corner patterns of each block.

2. Press the seam toward the 4/5 row.

Finishing Starburst Corners

1. The starburst corners are now in a triangle shape. Use a ruler and rotary cutter to trim, leaving an exact ¼″ seam allowance on the 2 short sides of the corner shape. Trim *only* the 2 short sides of the triangle shape for all 8 corner triangles of each block.

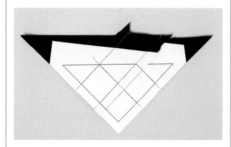

Trim all 8 starburst corner triangles on 2 short sides of triangle shape.

2. For each block, set aside 4 of the starburst corner triangles. These are the background triangles for the starburst block. You will trim the long edge of these triangles later.

3. Trim the long side of the 4 remaining starburst corner triangles. Use a ruler and rotary cutter to trim, leaving an exact ¼″ seam allowance.

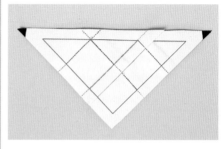

Trim 4 remaining starburst corner triangles on long side.

4. To make the starburst block's background corner squares, use the background half-square triangles and the trimmed starburst corner triangles. Lay a trimmed corner triangle on a background half-square triangle, right sides together, matching the long edge. Center the corner section on the background triangle as shown. Sew along the long edge, using a ¼″ seam. Press the seam allowance to the background.

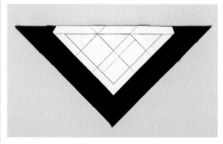

Center starburst corner triangle on large background half-square triangle, and stitch together.

Materials

Dark blue solid: ⅛ yard for star points

Salmon solid: ⅛ yard for star points

Green solid: Large scrap at least 2″ × 17″ or ⅛ yard for star points

Medium blue solid: ¼ yard for star and border

Purple solid: ¼ yard for star and binding

Red-violet solid: ¼ yard for star and border

Black solid: ⅔ yard for star, background, and border

Backing: ⅔ yard

Batting: 1 square 22″ × 22″

Cutting Instructions

Star and Background

Use the Cutting Chart, page 13, for the 5-row star with ¾″ diamond patches to cut the fabrics for the star and the background.

Borders

Inner Border

1. From the red-violet, cut 2 strips 1″ × width of fabric.

2. From the medium blue, cut 4 squares 1″ × 1″.

Outer Border

From the black, cut 2 strips 2½″ × width of fabric.

Binding

From the purple, cut 2 strips 2″ × width of fabric.

Preparing Patterns and Fabric

1. Make 8 copies of the pattern for the 5-row star with ¾″ patches, page 60. Cut and fold the patterns (see Basic Instructions, page 10).

2. Prepare the star fabric using the Cutting Chart, page 13, for the 5-row star, to determine the correct number of fabric pieces needed for each concentric ring. Label the fabric pieces with the number of the corresponding concentric ring.

Ring 1, star center: medium blue

Ring 2: red-violet

Ring 3: dark blue

Ring 4: black

Ring 5: medium blue

Ring 6: salmon

Ring 7: black

Ring 8: purple

Ring 9, star tips: green

Making 8 Star Points

1. Follow Steps 1–12 in Paper Piecing the Rows of the Star Point, pages 14–17, to paper piece the first set of rows. Orient the pattern as shown to paper piece the first set of rows.

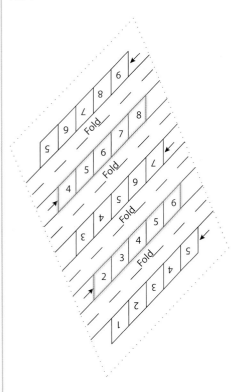

Orient pattern with diamond patch #9 up and diamond patch #1 down.

Save time by piecing multiple rows at once, using the pin placement method, page 15, for placing the fabrics.

2. Reorient the pattern as shown to paper piece the remaining 3 rows. Follow Steps 1–13 in Paper Piecing the Rows of the Star Point, pages 14–17, to complete the 3 remaining rows.

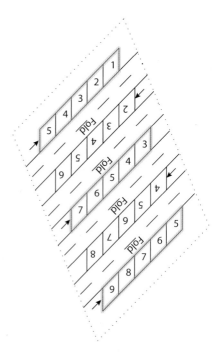

Orient pattern with diamond patch #1 up and diamond patch #9 down to paper piece 3 remaining rows.

3. Complete the star points (see Join the Paper-Pieced Rows, page 17, and Finish the Star Points, page 18).

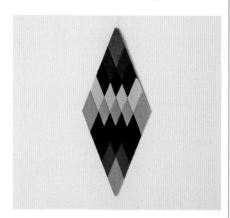

Completed star point for *Amish Star*

Completing the Star Block

1. Join the 8 completed star points together (see Assembling the Star, page 18).

2. Set in the background triangles and squares (see Adding a Background to Complete the Star Block, page 20).

Finishing

1. Press the block. Square up the completed star block to 13½″ × 13½″ (see Completing the Block, page 21).

2. Add the narrow red-violet border with blue corner squares (see Border with Corner Squares, page 25).

3. Add the black outer border (see Solid Border, page 25).

Layout and Assembly Diagram for *Amish Star*

4. Prepare the quilt top for finishing (see Removing the Glue and Paper, page 30).

5. Quilt, bind, and add a hanging sleeve and label (see Finishing the Quilt, page 25). *Amish Star* is machine quilted around the star with clear monofilament thread and hand quilted in the backgrounds and borders with pink, silk, 100-weight thread. Traditional Amish quilting designs of 8-pointed stars, tulips, and Amish squares are used. Amish quilt bindings have wider, straight-grain binding with overlapped corners rather than mitered corners. Consult a quilter's reference guide like *All About Quilting from A to Z* for this type of binding.

Beggar's Star, Lorraine Olsen, 2008.

I used the leftovers from a scrap exchange at our guild retreat to make this little charm quilt. The fabrics are randomly placed with no attention to color or value. I finished the edges with a scrappy border, pages 25–26, with 16 divisions.

Finished 5-row star block size: 9″ × 9″

Finished quilt size: 10½″ × 10½″

W hat fun to sit in my sewing room on a cold, wet day and play with the cheerful colors of my '30s scraps! This quilt is my miniature interpretation of the antique quilt that inspired this book. Value, rather than color, makes the design in this miniature. The detail of the little star points in the border adds to the illusion of a full-size quilt shrunk to a tiny size. I planned the colors and pieced each star point separately. The dark, medium, and light values in each concentric ring remain the same, and the colors change from star point to star point. The pattern calls for small amounts of each fabric, so this would be a perfect project on which to use charm packs, jelly rolls, or leftover reproduction scraps.

Materials

Assorted '30s reproduction prints in five different values: very dark, dark, medium, light, and very light: ½ yard total for star points and star point border

Light blue dot: ¼ yard for background

Light blue solid: ⅛ yard for border

Red print: ⅛ yard for binding

Backing: 1 square 15″ × 15″

Batting: 1 square 15″ × 15″

Cutting Instructions

Star

Use the Cutting Chart, page 13, for the 5-row star with ½″ diamond patches to cut the fabrics for the star and background.

Border

1. Use the Cutting Chart, page 12, for the 2-row star with ½″ diamond patches to cut the fabrics for the star points in the border. Cut enough pieces for 8 star points, but do not cut any background pieces.

2. From the light blue solid, cut 1 strip 1¼″ × width of fabric. Cut the strip into 4 rectangles 1¼″ × 9½″.

Binding

From the red print, cut 2 strips 1½″ × width of fabric.

Preparing Patterns and Fabric

1. Make 8 copies of the pattern for the 5-row star with ½″ patches, page 62. Cut and fold the patterns (see Basic Instructions, page 10).

2. Prepare the star fabrics using the Cutting Chart, page 13, for the 5-row star, to determine the correct number of fabric pieces needed for each concentric ring. Plan the colors and fabrics of each star point separately. Use the same values in each concentric ring from star point to star point. See Fabric Value, page 9, for help in sorting the fabric scraps into values.

Label the fabric pieces with the number of the corresponding concentric ring.

Ring 1, star center: dark   Ring 6: very dark

Ring 2: medium   Ring 7: medium

Ring 3: light   Ring 8: light

Ring 4: dark   Ring 9, star tips: dark

Ring 5: very light

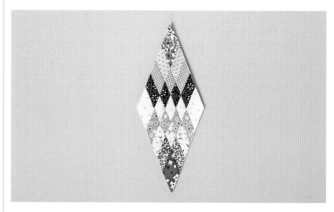

Notice range of values in completed star point for *Rainy Day Star*.

tip   Many '30s prints are in the medium-value range. Look for other fabrics in very dark and very light values that harmonize with the '30s prints. Green, red, and royal blue prints are good choices for the very dark value. Use pastels on white backgrounds for the very light value.

Making 8 Star Points

Complete the 8 star points using the same instructions for Making 8 Star Points in *Amish Star*, pages 55–56.

Completing the Star Block

1. Join the star points together (see Assembling the Star, page 18).

2. Set in the background triangles and squares (see Adding a Background to Complete the Star Block, page 20).

3. Press the block. Square up the completed star block to 9½″ × 9½″ (see Completing the Block, page 21).

Border

Star Points

1. Make 8 copies of the pattern for the 2-row star with ½″ patches, page 12. Cut and fold the patterns (see Basic Instructions, page 10).

2. Use 3 values of fabric on the little star points:

Ring 1: dark

Ring 2: light

Ring 3: medium

Make 8 star points (see Preparing Patterns and Fabric, page 11, and Making Star Points, page 14).

3. Press and trim the 2-row star points, but do not sew them together.

Border Assembly

1. Use the 2-row star points and the 1¼″ × 9½″ rectangles of light blue solid to assemble the border (see Star Points Border, pages 29–30).

2. Sew the borders to the star block.

Layout and Assembly Diagram for *Rainy Day Star*

Finishing

1. Prepare the quilt top for finishing (see Removing the Glue and Paper, page 30).

 Trim all the seams to ⅛″ after stitching if the star is to be hand quilted.

2. Quilt, bind, and add a hanging sleeve and label (see Finishing the Quilt, page 25). *Rainy Day Star* is entirely hand quilted with grey, 100-weight silk thread. Quilt the star in the ditch and quilt feathered rosettes in the background. The border has a quilted rope design.

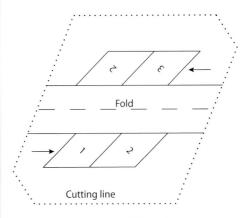

Fold

Cutting line

Pattern for 2-row star with ½″ patches

Little Christmas Tree Ornaments, Lorraine Olsen, 2008.

The pattern for the little star points in *Rainy Day Star* is the perfect size to finish into little star blocks and make ornaments for a Christmas tree.

patterns

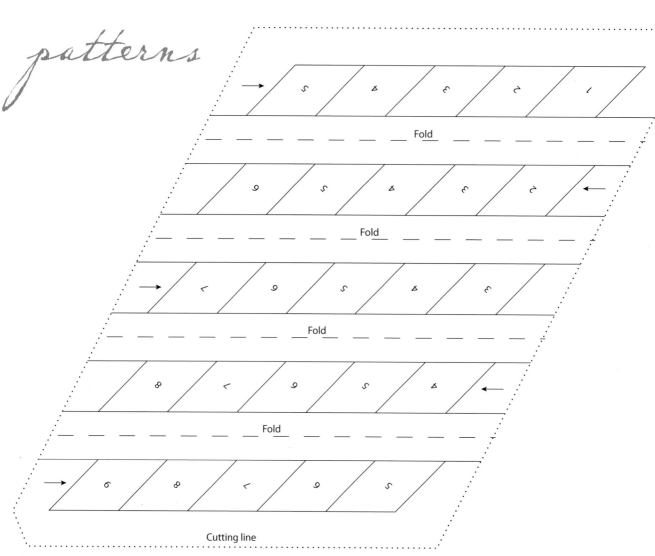

Pattern for 5-row star with ¾″ patches

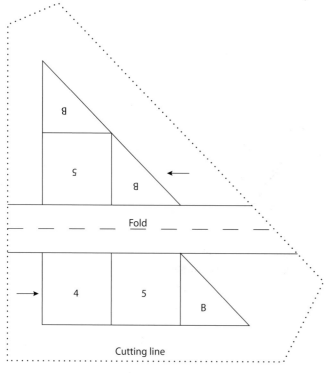

Pattern for Starburst corner

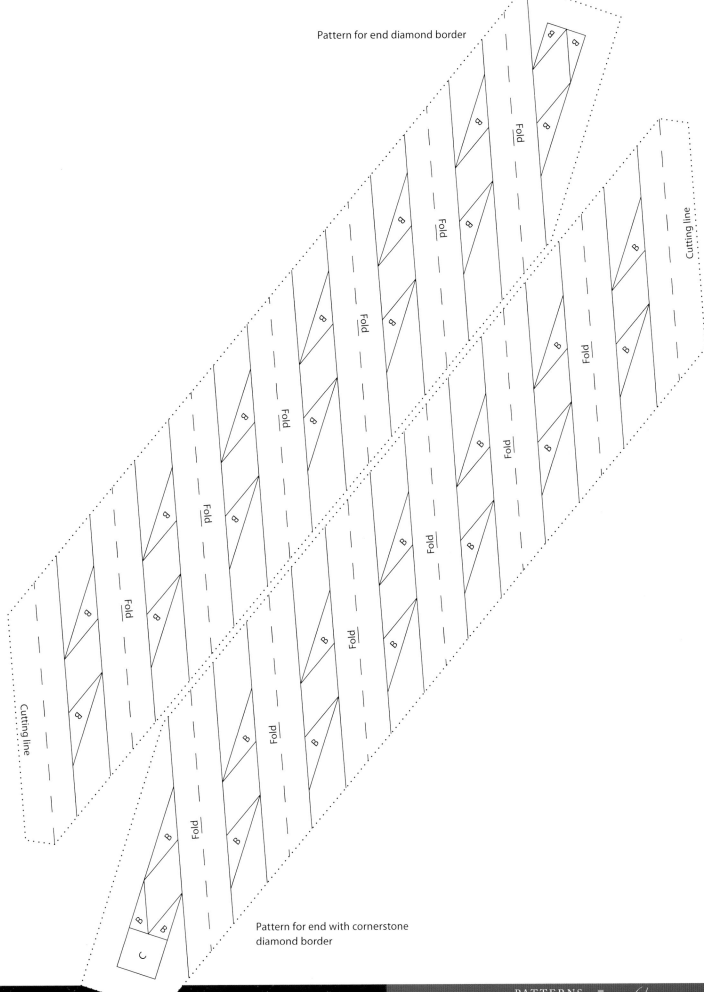

Pattern for end diamond border

Cutting line

Fold

Fold

Fold

Fold

Fold

Fold

Fold

Fold

Fold

Fold

Fold

Cutting line

Pattern for end with cornerstone
diamond border

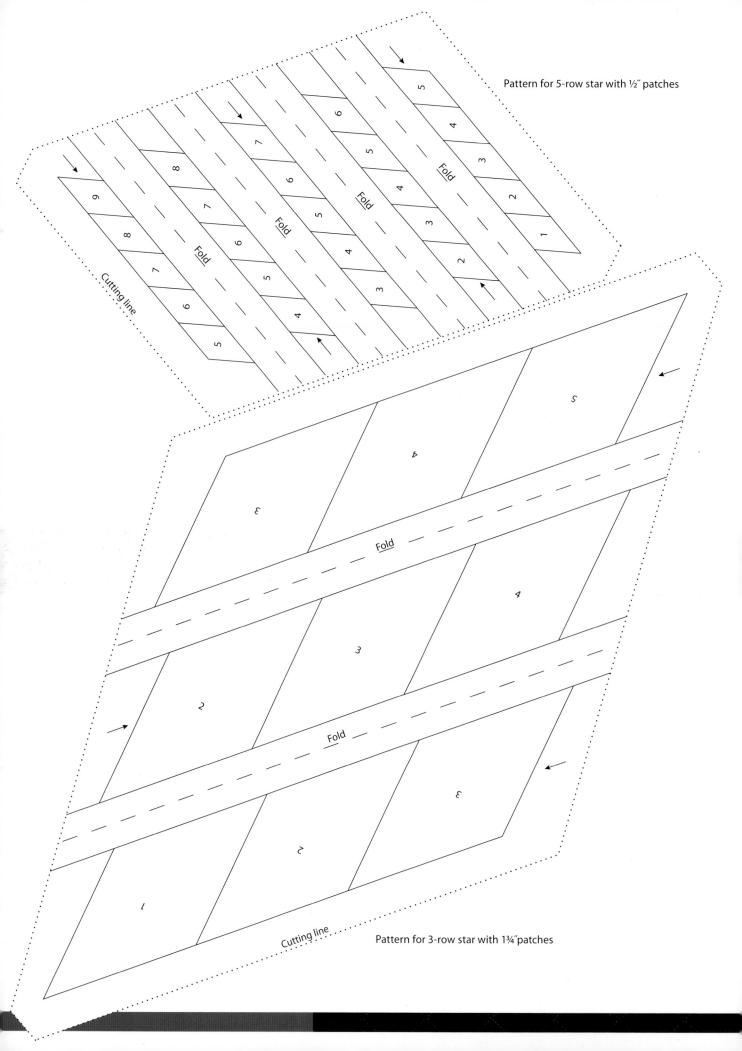

Pattern for 5-row star with ½″ patches

Pattern for 3-row star with 1¾″ patches

resources

FOR QUILTING SUPPLIES:

Clothworks
6250 Stanley Avenue South
Seattle, WA 98108
www.clothworks-fabric.com

Creative Impressions
1485 Garden of the Gods Road, Unit 100
Colorado Springs, CO 80907
www.creativeimpressions.com

Dharma Trading Co.
P.O. Box 150916
San Rafael, CA 94915
www.dharmatrading.com

Dritz/Prym
www.dritz.com

The Electric Quilt Company
419 Gould Street, Suite 2
Bowling Green, OH 43402
www.electricquilt.com

Fairfield Processing
P.O. Box 1130
Danbury, CT 06813
www.poly-fil.com

Just Another Button Company
116 W. Market Street
Troy, IL 62294
www.justanotherbuttoncompany.com

Mary Arden of England
14 Westover Avenue
Stamford, CT 06902

P & B Textiles
1580 Gilbreth Road
Burlingame, CA 94010
www.pbtex.com

RJR Fabrics
www.rjrfabrics.com

Sulky
P.O. Box 494129
Port Charlotte, FL 33949
www.sulky.com

Superior Threads
87 East 2580 South
St. George, UT 84790
www.superiorthreads.com

Timeless Treasures Fabrics
483 Broadway
New York, NY 10013
www.ttfabrics.com

YLI
1439 Dave Lyle Blvd. #16C
Rock Hill, SC 29730
www.ylicorp.com

about the author

Lorraine grew up learning sewing and quilting from her mother and grandmothers. Her love of fabric was apparent early as she rescued discarded scraps and used them to make clothes and quilts for her dolls. She received her first sewing machine on her ninth birthday to keep her from monopolizing her mother's.

She has always enjoyed making clothing and utility quilts for her family. Lorraine fell in love with patchwork after her children were in school, and she started collecting patchwork patterns. She discovered miniatures after seeing some little quilts at a local quilt show, and just had to try a few. Her little quilts won prizes at local shows and fairs. Lorraine now competes in national quilt shows and has a miniature quilt in the Museum of the American Quilter's Society permanent collection.

She still loves rescuing scraps and has a large collection of small pieces of fabric. She uses her collection to make small reproduction quilts. She has recently learned how to dye fabric and looks for ways to use all the hand-dyed fabric in her quilts.

Lorraine Olsen
Photo by Cullam Olsen

Lorraine lives in Springfield, Missouri, with her husband and teenage son. Her married daughter and son visit often. Lorraine enjoys being outdoors and walking the local Ozark trails with her family.

Little Lone Star Quilts is Lorraine's first book. For more information about Lorraine's work, visit her website at www.lorraineolsenquilts.com

Great Titles *from* C&T PUBLISHING

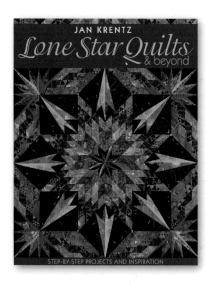

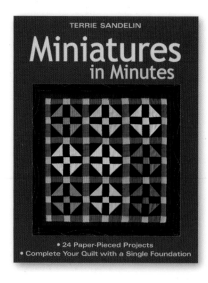

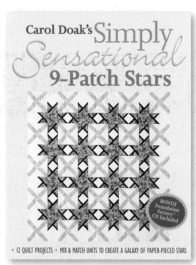

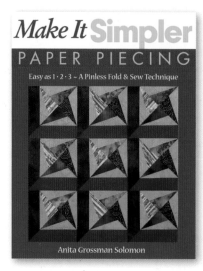

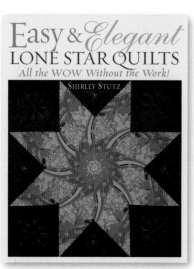

Available at your local retailer or **www.ctpub.com** *or* **800.284.1114**

For a list of other fine books from C&T Publishing,
ask for a free catalog:

C&T PUBLISHING, INC.

P.O. Box 1456

Lafayette, CA 94549

(800) 284-1114

Email: ctinfo@ctpub.com

Website: www.ctpub.com

C&T Publishing's professional photography services are now available
to the public. Visit us at www.ctmediaservices.com.

For quilting supplies:

COTTON PATCH

1025 Brown Ave.

Lafayette, CA 94549

Store: (925) 284-1177

Mail order: (925) 283-7883

Email: CottonPa@aol.com

Website: www.quiltusa.com

Note: Fabrics used in the quilts shown may not be currently
available, as fabric manufacturers keep most fabrics in
print for only a short time.